Young, Fun

&

Financially Free

Live the Good Life Now and

Build a Kick-Ass Future

Leanna Haakons

ISBN 13: 978-0-9988546-3-2
ISBN 10: 0-9988546-3-8

If you would like to publish sections of this book, please contact the publisher for permission.

Published by: Celebrity Expert Author
http://celebrityexpertauthor.com

Canadian Address:
1108 - 1155 The High Street,
Coquitlam, BC, Canada
V3B.7W4
Phone: (604) 941-3041
Fax: (604) 944-7993

US Address:
1300 Boblett Street
Unit A-218
Blaine, WA 98230
Phone: (866) 492-6623
Fax: (250) 493-6603

Dedication

TO ALL OF THE family and friends who have supported and encouraged me in my madness. I know I'm crazy, thank you for loving me for it! And to every person I've ever taken out to coffee, drinks, a meal, hopped on a flight to meet, or had a call with when our busy world's kept us apart, you have educated and inspired me to get to this point. You may not have known your influence on me at the time, however, you have been so truly instrumental in helping me become the knowledgeable woman I am today. I can't thank or appreciate you enough. Strong mentors are the backbone of individual success and I am so honored to have each of you in my life. I considered listing you all by name, but it would have been way too long! From the bottom of my heart, thank you.

~ "The Hawk"

About WE

WE MAKES DOING GOOD, doable. WE empowers change with resources that create sustainable impact. We do this through domestic programs like WE Schools and internationally through WE Villages. For two decades, WE Villages has been engineering an international development model to end poverty. It works. It's proven. It's scalable. It's not a handout or a single solution, but a combination of key interventions that empower a community to help themselves. Our core mission is empowerment. In North America, we empower people to create positive change around them. WE Villages applies the same philosophy in developing countries, when our local staff work with rural villages and regional governments to support, teach and empower people within our five Pillars of Impact: Education, Water, Health, Food, Opportunity.

Children can only attend school if their parents have the financial means and time to invest in their education and basic health. Through the opportunity pillar, we teach parents, often mothers, skills such as animal husbandry, to help them generate income, accrue savings and ensure sustainability. Through a mix of engaging the local government and developing alternative income programs, we help our WE Villages partner communities reach a level of self-sufficiency within an average of five years. As of today, 30,000 women have been provided with the tools for economic self-sufficiency. And this has had a direct impact on the health and welfare of their families and their communities. Enabling women, specifically, to become earners is smart economics—it improves the financial and health outcomes of the entire community.

By purchasing and reading this book you will not only learn how to become financially free yourself, you will be helping others around the world become financially independent as well.

Thank you for supporting the WE movement!

Contents

Chapter 4

Chapter 5

Chapter 6
Sorry, but Notorious B.I.G. Had It Wrong—Mo' Money = Less problems! 81

Chapter 7
Investing Basics: Now that You Have Some Dough, Let's Make It Grow! 93

Chapter 8
Getting to Ground Zero: Paying off Your Debt and Restoring Your Credit 111

Introduction

"Money is not the most important thing in the world. Love is.
Fortunately, I love money."
~ Jackie Mason

HAVE YOU WONDERED HOW you're ever going to get ahead and be able to live the lifestyle you want without making more money? Sure, making more money is great, but you don't necessarily need more than what you already have. You just need to put it to work wisely!

My friends and family have been asking me since I was twenty-one how I own a home in the most expensive area of Vancouver, drive a great car, wear designer items, travel freely, and do all the things that I do. Most people probably thought I had some sort of trust fund, but that's far from the truth! I'm going to share the secrets of how I did it, and it all started on a 35K CAD annual salary (~27K USD), which was way less than the people questioning me were making! It's no mystery. I've been able to live a great life on a shoe-string budget and it's allowed me to become financially free from a young age.

Contrary to many beliefs, money is not the root of all evil; money is an incredible tool.

Becoming financially free and living an abundant life isn't simply about getting rich or being what is quintessentially measured as successful. It's about making strategic

choices in the way you save and spend your money, prioritizing your true values and the things you desire to achieve
most. For example, small changes like saying "no thanks" to
going out for lunch with office friends at $15/day x 22 days/
month = $330/month x 12 months = $3960/year to invest, or
a pretty sweet trip to Europe! What's the bigger priority to
you? Lunches out or traveling?

It's also about putting your money to work for you,
allowing it to grow for future goals through investing. A little bit of knowledge goes a long way. Whether your dream
lifestyle entails buying a home, traveling four weeks a year,
paying for your children's education, working part-time only,
or upgrading to a fancy new car every few years, all goals and
dreams are met by following the same guidelines and principles, starting with living in the right *money mindset.*

By being in the right money mindset, you know where
you're headed, what your priorities and goals are, and how
you're going to get there. You've recognized how important
it is to live a life free from the effects of money stress like
lack of sleep, health issues, your children growing up with
poor money skills, and the general worries that paycheck to
paycheck living and bad debt causes.

What does your dream lifestyle look like? How many
days a week do you want to work? Do you want to travel?
Own a home? How are you going to achieve these things?
There are *Four Key Steps to Reaching Your Financial Nirvana*;
I'll show you what they are here.

While other kids were geeking out on video games, I
became the world's biggest financial nerd. My friends
thought I was crazy! From the age of eighteen, I was teaching myself about the stock market, investing, and personal
finance through reading books, rapidly taking notes while
watching TV shows like Jim Cramer's *Mad Money* on
CNBC every day after school, and pestering older friends
and mentors who were working in the industry with my

keener questions. I've been working and building my network of financial experts all over the world for over twelve
years. Whenever I could, I took people out to coffee, lunch,
and drinks to learn more. I've paid for many flights and trips
out of my own pocket to meet with people I was intrigued by
and knew I could learn from.

Nowadays, I'm the queen of podcasts and videos, incredible free resources for information on personal finance,
investing, business, and just about anything else. I recommend that everyone listen to podcasts. There are thousands of
great podcasts on all kinds of subjects. I listen to at least ten
per day on double speed while I'm walking my dog, driving,
running errands, and getting ready in the morning. What an
awesome way to learn while getting other things done. (Did
I mention I'm also the queen of multitasking?)

My genuine interest and hyper-eagerness to get ahead
in my financial life has always been my biggest personal and
professional passion. I've stayed dedicated to my own money
education through practical experience working in the field
of finance while furthering my formal education through
obtaining my business degree, financial regulatory licensing,
and other post-secondary ventures in multiple jurisdictions
including Canada, the United States, the United Kingdom,
and Europe. This sounds like a lot of schooling, however,
being the money nerd that I am, I thrived on every second
of it and hope I can pass on some of that knowledge to you.

There have been many ups and downs and hard lessons
learned along the way. Living the dream is no easy feat and
can often seem like an uphill battle; as with most rewards,
there is risk associated. Most of us were not provided with
basic financial education in school, so it can be hard to know
where to look for information, and to stay motivated on your
financial journey.

It doesn't matter if you have zero education or experience
in finance. NEWSFLASH! Many people have little to no

clue what they're doing with their money. Whether it's budgeting, investing, saving, or spending you have to start with the basics. This includes knowing what you're fighting for.

The pace of life is very different now than it was fifty years ago, as is the cost of education, real estate values, and salaries to support the ever-increasing price of urban living. Just trying to keep up with your job and family commitments alone is hard enough. The daunting thought of your finances (something most people have no experience with professionally, as well as no personal interest) can be overwhelming. In this book, I break down some of the basics so you can get on the right path to taking action.

What's been holding you back? We'll consider different ideas you might have about money, like how your parents thought and spoke to you about money growing up, who you should or shouldn't be depending on (a partner is not a plan!), and any other inhibitions or roadblocks which may have held you back so far.

If you're feeling a little nervous about tackling a subject you've been too afraid to even think about for the greater portion of your life, that's totally normal. You might not feel 100 percent ready to dig deep right now, but the truth is you're never going to feel completely ready to go for it, no one does. The longer you wait, the bigger your money issues will get, and the more complicated life becomes. Waiting for the right time to get things straightened out won't work either, as there's never going to be a "right time"; you don't want to wait until you hit rock bottom. Finding more excuses to procrastinate about tackling the most important aspect of your personal independence won't do you any favors.

I was lucky enough to be born into an affluent family of self-made entrepreneurs who came from humble means, and openly discussed money and how to best make, spend, and save it. Although I was given many opportunities as a child, none of my family members or relatives worked in finance, and my passion for investing came purely from my own interest.

For over a decade, I've traveled through the world of finance knocking on doors until they opened, soaking up as much knowledge and experience as I could. To all the parents and future parents reading this book—you are shaping the way your kids will handle money for the rest of their lives. What our parents teach us about the value of a dollar or any other life lessons, is what we instinctively know and will likely practice as adults.

Do you want to create your own legacy and one for your children? Give them the gift of learning how to be financially independent so they can live a life representative of their own values and priorities. Together we will explore these and other lessons, and let them be just that—lessons, rather than roadblocks holding you back from what you truly want.

The biggest problem is that unfortunately most financial marketing and media is rigged against you. The system has you programmed to do exactly the wrong thing and puts you on the fast track to being broke for life. If you don't have the basic knowledge of how to work the system in your favor, you might end up being out of luck.

There are a couple of other key problems I see in today's society holding people back from financial greatness. Firstly, the lack of financial literacy being taught in schools is making it difficult for young people to know how to manage their money from the get-go. Secondly, the world's focus on social media and online information has taken over. This has caused a constant culture of comparison, instant gratification, and a keeping up with the Joneses mentality. The sad truth is that most of what you see on social media is fake. Financial envy and trying to keep up with the lifestyles of the rich and famous in the best moments of their heavily sponsored, promoted, and filtered lives is a losing battle, and a fast track to financial destruction.

On the other hand, you might be in the workforce making your way up the corporate ladder or going the entrepreneurial route, accumulating money as you progress in your career, and you're wondering what to do with it. This is great! I'm going to give you some ideas as to how you can find a solution to your saving and investing headaches by increasing your **Return on Investment (ROI)** to make your money grow! You should be excited about your investing future! The basics aren't difficult to understand, you just need someone to teach you in the right way.

Depending on your age, personality, income, and level of risk tolerance, some investments will be better suited than others to helping you meet your lifestyle goals. Your money is a tool that should be working for you. The positive power of **compounding interest**, the ability for your money to make more money for you, is an incredible thing and a concept important to understand. You don't need to be a millionaire or billionaire to be financially free, but you do need to know what you truly want, why you want it, and how much money you're going to need to get there.

This is where the **warning** about credit cards and consumer debt comes in. Of the most detrimental to your credit score, highest cost, and most painful kind of debts, credit card debt is at the top of the list. Whether you got your first card in your twenties and the ability to pay with plastic for school expenses and nights out with friends got out of control, or your cost of living is so high that you're putting your family's monthly expenses on credit, credit card interest rates (typically anywhere from 15-29%) and compounding interest charges get so out of control that it can be tough to get out of the downward spiral without guidance and support.

Example: Did you know that if you spend $5,000 on your credit card this month, with an interest rate of 22%, and don't pay the whole thing off right away, **it would cost you approximately nine times as much after ten years**? That's right, $5,000 on a credit card today will equal a balance owing of over $44,000 in ten years!

If you're coming from a place of debt, I'm going to show you a couple of tried and true ways to get yourself out of it. Having the confidence in knowing that you can get out of debt and other financial woes—no matter where you're starting from today—is so important. Work toward having a fresh new mindset about money and how to use it as a tool to fund your future.

On the topic of wants, needs, and instant gratification, an important part of your overall financial picture and where to get started, is assessing your spending power and habits. Savings fits into this equation as well, as saving money doesn't have to equal suffering and a loss of quality of life. Preservation, not deprivation is the name of the game! Learn how to spend wisely to get what you need and want now while saving for your future. I'll share some of my best tricks for living the high life while spending less than half of what my friends waste.

This book will walk you through many of the crucial aspects of how to prepare for life's unforeseen events, and how to recover from your mistakes. Life is tough sometimes, I know it all too well, some of which you'll read about here. It's the struggles that make every single one of us stronger and better aligned for future success. In particular, I hope Chapter 10 will show you that if you have access to this book right now, no matter who you are or where you came from, you have the resources it takes to reach your financial goals. With a certain amount of grit and commitment, you will get there. All you have to do is make the commitment to get started, go at your own pace, and be excited for what your future holds.

It's never too late, or early, to start living the life of your dreams. You have a decision to make now. Are you going to stay on the path to going broke? Or are you going to wake up from this financial hazing that society has given you and start creating your own plan? If you're not going to wake up, best of luck. You'll make the banks and credit card companies richer. If you're ready for a change, let's do this! I'll show you how learning about money doesn't have to be so serious and boring, and can actually be fun and exciting! More importantly, you now have the chance to learn what your money can provide for you and your family. Best of all, you get to live the good life without sacrifice. You in?

Chapter 1

The #1 Thing People Do that Screws up Their Finances: Step 1 on Your Path to Financial Nirvana

"Too many people spend money they haven't earned, to buy things they don't want, to impress people they don't like."
~ Will Smith

WHEN I TALK TO my friends, I get this sad sense of hopelessness about money and what it can do to (not FOR) your future and lifestyle overall; let me explain. Many believe they'll never be able to own a home, travel as much as they want, create their own hours, get out of credit card debt, pay off their student loans, etc. In this chapter, I'll explain how these things aren't true and why.

You might believe that in order to be wealthy you need to be born with a silver spoon in your mouth or marry rich, and that's simply not true. A partner is not a plan! Neither is a trust fund or inheritance you expect to receive in the future. You need to be able to depend on your own knowledge of money and how the financial system works to either make your own money, or preserve what you've been lucky enough to receive from others.

Have you ever met or heard of a wealthy family whose money has disappeared through the generations? Family wealth disappears all the time, and it's not something you can necessarily bank on to fund your future. If you don't teach your kids the fundamentals of money before they start falling down the rabbit hole as adults, your family legacy could be in jeopardy.

My parents openly discussed money and made sure I knew the value of a dollar by showing me how hard they worked and that I was expected to do the same. Handouts and bailouts will only get your children to the next situation where they're asking you to open your wallet. Instead, teach them how to find solutions to their problems as if they were independent adults.

Most people have made mistakes with money, myself included. If this is the case, learning from your mistakes and changing your habits is going to be your biggest asset going forward. Ever heard of those people who win the lottery and are broke within a few years? Whether you're starting from ground zero or getting **back to black** (out of debt), it's all possible; but before you get there you need to lay the ground-work to make sure the new insights you'll read about in this book are implemented properly and stick.

It's simple to create wealth if you have the right infor-mation; the wrong info can quickly destroy your wealth and future.

One of my biggest frustrations throughout my young adulthood and career in finance thus far is when friends, family, acquaintances, and even strangers think that the rea-son why I'm so good with money is because I was educated and work in the field of finance. Absolutely, it's helped to understand a lot of investing theories, products, econom-ics, portfolio management concepts, and other important aspects of financial planning; but the real wisdom behind how to be good with money was ingrained in me from a young age through my family's teachings, as well as through my own determination to achieve my lifestyle goals and live the way I want, without being under the thumb of money stress. Getting to this stage is what I call being in the right **money mindset**.

It's so much easier to get in the right money mindset if you actively think about what you truly want out of life, how you want to live, and knowing that with the right mindset you can achieve these things. It might sound cheesy and all hocus pocus to think you can achieve your financial goals with the right mindset, but through putting the tools in this book to work and staying dedicated to your commitment to yourself, you can actually make your dreams a reality. It doesn't come easy, but nothing worth it in life does in my opinion.

Stop Feeling Hopeless

One of the biggest reasons I wanted to write this book was to explain to all those in my life, and those I hope to inspire and meet in the future, why I see so many young adults and intelligent people in general struggling with their finances. Being good with money and allowing it to create the life you desire has literally nothing to do with how much money you make, how smart you are, or how hard you work—nothing at all. I can't stress this enough. It drives me nuts to hear my friends complaining that they don't make enough money to do this or that or the other. Of course, if you're on a tight income and you have obligations to your family, like children or other dependents, you absolutely have more responsibilities on your plate than others. However, that doesn't mean you can't get yourself in the right money mindset to do the absolute most you can with what you have—and enjoy it—while allowing your wealth to grow through investing and making wise decisions.

Making choices about our money is all about giving

security to ourselves and those we're responsible for, as well as using our money to live our lives in a way that makes us happy, inspired, and money stress-free. **The #1 thing people do to screw up their finances is not believing in the power they have over their own money mindset**, setting themselves up for failure. Your money should bring you confidence, security, and enjoyment. Every road has bumps and detours along the way; you might have a significant amount of debt at this stage to get off your back, with some examples more extreme than others. However, I promise that with some simple tools and wrapping your head around the fact that your money can actually help you be more confident and happy, rather than stressed and worried, you will find a solution.

Ignorance isn't bliss! The first step toward financial freedom is having the belief that **you can** take control of your money and your life.

Identify Your Weaknesses

Now, for those who haven't yet figured this out or aren't quite in the right mindset with your finances, let's take a look at the two primary traps I see people falling into. You might not fit into either of these two categories, although it's more likely than not that you can somehow relate.

To figure out the root of your own financial insecurities and what is causing you to be so stressed about money, identifying key weaknesses when it comes to your money mindset is top priority. To do this, a basic analysis of your month-to-month income and expenses is a simple way to pinpoint some issues which might seem minor at the time when you swipe your credit card, pay your rent or mortgage, process your car and insurance payments, or go out for drinks and dinner with friends after work. However, overall it can add up to major spending patterns, which is the root of the problems in your financial life.

Why do you spend all your money every month? Where is it all going? Are all of these things absolutely necessary? Are they providing you the happiness you want and deserve? Have you ever truly looked at where every dollar goes that you make? Most importantly—is this spending fulfilling your deepest desires, or are there bigger priorities you truly want for your life that these spending habits might be holding you back from? If you're unsure, keep reading.

> ## Chapter Bonus:
> Go to the **Young, Fun & Financially Free website** at **www.youngfunfree.com** to get your personal **Identify My Weaknesses** worksheet.

Two Types of Financial Hopelessness

Give Your Head a Shake and Get out of Your Own Way (Type 1)

I have met so many amazingly intelligent and creative people in my life. I've interviewed and worked with doctors, aerospace engineers, architects, writers, musicians, and lots of other successful people in their fields who, for some reason, have not much to show for it. For many, they worked so hard during their schooling years that once they broke out into the working world and started making a significant income, they didn't know what to do with it. The most natural mode of instant gratification they got from this money was to spend and enjoy it (in the short term).

Not for lack of ambitions, many highly intelligent people aren't good with money. Why? Because they were never taught how to be, had natural interests in other fields, were never influenced by people that were good with money growing up, or perhaps just never cared until it became a problem. Too little, too late, as they say—well, not anymore. It's never too late to fix your **confused spending** habits and learn the right tools for financial success. This is actually the most hopeful type of financially hopeless person if you consider yourself an intelligent person with an income who simply doesn't know how to manage it. For that matter, you actually don't have to be an intelligent person at all to learn how to manage your money and make it work for you. The basics are simple. Once you determine what you want your life to look like, not just your bank accounts and investments, it's fairly easy to pull together a plan to make that lifestyle a reality.

These are the only two requirements to making your financial dreams a reality:

1) Willingness to learn (and earn).

2) Have a job that pays you something.

Break the Cycle (Type 2)

Depending on where and with whom you grew up as your influencers and mentors, you might naturally have a very different outlook on money and life than I do. As a child and throughout my twenties, I was surrounded by a family of successful self-made entrepreneurs in engineering and real estate (not finance), a mother and grandma who were the best deal finders you've ever met (until me—thanks, Mom!), and too many financial industry moguls to count. Whether you grew up rich, poor, in between, or a mix of all of them, you can choose—yes, it's a choice—what you want your money mindset to be and what you prioritize in your life when it comes to your financial and lifestyle goals.

Through all the financially successful people I've met in my time so far, the most incredibly inspiring stories come from the millionaires and billionaires—world renowned entrepreneurs and those who are financially free no matter what their net worth is—who came from backgrounds where they were forced to overcome adversity to become who they are today. They were forced to look beyond the social norm of what they knew growing up, what maybe every other person who had known them thought they would be when they grew up. They envisioned what they wanted their life to look like and made it happen. Rather than be intimidated by wealth and money, feeling destined to a life of credit card debt, never-ending student loans, social assistance, and everything else they'd been exposed to, they changed their **money mindset** to allow their dreams to drive them to get where they are today. It didn't have anything to do with how much money they wanted to make, but everything to do with how they wanted their lives to look and feel. In no way do I mean to undermine the challenges that so many people and families around the world experience, although I do hope to inspire and teach you how to live on your own terms.

To be inspired by some of the most successful people in finance and otherwise who have overcome their own adversity and strife, check out the **incredible interviews** I've done and posted on my **YouTube Channel** by visiting **http://bit. ly/leannahawk**, or search for "Leanna Haakons" on YouTube. I will show you that no matter where you came from, the destination is up to you.

The Grass Isn't Always Greener—Beware of Social Media Lifestyle Traps

I resisted social media for a long time, as I like to keep my personal life private and find so much about social media super annoying (all my friends are laughing at me right now), but I finally got social media accounts in 2017. I knew the only way I would be able to reach a massive amount of people to teach them about financial wellness and empowerment would be to utilize social media platforms. Sadly, some of the things I always believed about social media are more prevalent now that I see it every day. Although I have seen some wonderfully inspiring profiles that highlight reality, most of it is so incredibly fake. I'm not talking from a physical beauty standpoint (although I'm sure the cat's out of the bag on that already), but the lifestyles of people on social media. Photo shoots on private jets, yachts, runways, galas, shopping sprees, etc. this is not real life for most of us. These are professional, promotional photo shoots for a reason; it's just business. I too post professional photos on social media, and there's nothing wrong with that; the key is being aware when looking at people's lifestyles on Instagram, Facebook, and the like, that although everyone has incredible experiences from time to time, this isn't real daily life; these images are definitely not what you should be comparing your own life to. In fact, comparing your life to those on social media can be hugely detrimental to your self-confidence and financial situation.

Living in financial envy trying to keep up with the Joneses is impossible, nor should you be living your life to someone else's standards. Live it for yourself! Who cares how many photos you share on social media? Be happy with your own life and live it. In this book I talk a lot about setting your financial goals and determining what your dream lifestyle looks like. There's a great one-minute video on CNBC's *Make It* about how a 36-year-old schoolteacher became a millionaire. He didn't do this by pretending to be on yachts and jets with bikini clad models on Instagram. He did it by being frugal, investing his savings smartly, exercising his mind and body and making good decisions. ***Check out the video on the "YFF" (Young, Fun, Free) website!***

Chapter Bonus:

Want to calculate when you'll become a millionaire by saving $500 or $1000 or $10 a month? Check out the **Millionaire Calculator on the YFF website**.

Dig Deep: If Financial Nirvana is where you want to be but you haven't got there yet, why not?

Summary

In this chapter we've discussed how simple it can be, regardless of your background, to create wealth and live the lifestyle you dream of if you commit to learn, earn, and adjust your habits. So much of this ties into analyzing your own financial situation given your responsibilities, income, priorities, and, most importantly, weaknesses. Once you can identify the habits and patterns that are keeping you from living the life you want, it's so much easier to see the light at the end of the tunnel and get there. Scrolling through the lifestyles of the fake and fabulous on social media won't get you there; believing in yourself will. In the next chapter we'll discuss dreaming big, setting your lifestyle goals, and how it all starts and ends with you. As the saying goes, if you don't believe in yourself, no one else will either.

My Two Cents:

- You don't have to have a business degree, financial career, or know a lot about investing to live with financial freedom. But it helps to have someone guide the way.

- **Ignorance isn't bliss!** The first step toward financial freedom is having the confidence in knowing you can take control of your money and your life. You must be in the right **money mindset** to allow your money to work for you, no matter what your income.

- The **#1 thing people do to screw up their finances** is not believing in the power they have over their own money mindset. Financial despair is not your destiny!

- The first thing to do when looking at your own financial situation is to **identify your weaknesses.** What's holding you back? Download the worksheet from the website to figure yours out.

- No matter how hard you work or how smart you are, neither of those will ever make you financially free.

- **Two types of financial hopelessness**: Confused spenders and those who need to break the cycle.

- The grass isn't always greener—**beware of social media lifestyle traps**. Trying to keep up with the social media Joneses is a fast track to ruining your financial future.

- **Believe in yourself!** In the next chapter we'll talk about dreaming big and how setting lifestyle goals starts with believing in yourself and knowing your strengths!

Chapter Bonuses:

1) Go to **www.youngfunfree.com** to get your personal **Identify my Weaknesses** worksheet.

2) Want to calculate when you'll become a millionaire by saving $500 or $1000 or $10 a month? Check out the **Millionaire Calculator** on the YFF website.

NOTE: Consider these Chapter Bonus exercises throughout the book your *good life work.* They can be downloaded on the Young, Fun & Financially Free website. (Homework to get you started on your dream life!)

Chapter 2

Knowing Your WHY and WHAT: Step 2 on Your Path to Financial Nirvana

*"If you think nobody cares if you're alive,
try missing a couple of car payments."*
~ Earl Wilson

NOW THAT YOU KNOW you're going to be okay and it doesn't matter where you're starting from, hopefully you're beginning to have confidence in knowing that you can do this. You're going to love this chapter; it's a fun one because now we get to talk about what you want in your life and why. What does success mean to you? Success in your career, with your money, family, physically, spiritually, and emotionally? Let's talk about why **get rich quick schemes don't work,** won't make you happy, and where to go next.

Want to "Get Rich Quick?" Then this Book Isn't for You

I'm not a fan of the word *rich*. Everyone interprets the meaning of rich and success in different ways. As a woman coming from many years in the finance and investing world, you might think I'd write a book about how to become rich or how to make your first million or how to retire by thirty, but to me these are all meaningless mass media ploys. When I was eighteen and had my first job in the stock market, I said I wanted to retire by the time I was thirty. Well, I'll be thirty by the time this book is released so that sure didn't happen, and now I wouldn't have it any other way. If you're looking for a get rich quick scheme to make a certain dollar amount, or to create massive wealth purely in the monetary sense, this book is not for you. I like to take a much more balanced approach to financial and personal life goals. Living a full, rich, happy life has so many more aspects than your net worth (your **net worth** is the amount by which your assets exceed all your liabilities).

In this day and age of positive corporate culture, life/work balance, health and fitness, and so many other elements that encompass a well-rounded, joyous life, a get rich quick method isn't going to be of much help when it comes to achieving your overall lifestyle goals. Don't be fooled! Getting rich quick might seem like a nice option (A.K.A the easy path), but, just like those social media Joneses, the 99 percent fake factor hits hard. Nothing is worse than wasting more time, money, effort, and sleep over another failed attempt at taking the easy way out. I'm not telling you it'll be easy to get out of whatever financial crisis you happen to be in, but I can guarantee you it will be worth it.

No matter how much money you have or earn, unless you know how to keep it you'll never get ahead. It's the reason why many professional athletes, lottery winners, and celebrities declare bankruptcy within five years of the end of their earnings.

What is Financial Nirvana? Hint: It's Where You Want to Be but for Some Reason You're Not There Yet

Living in your own state of Financial Nirvana means making the absolute most of your money, allowing you to meet your lifestyle goals to live a fulfilling and abundant life.

Living in Financial Nirvana really comes down to what kind of lifestyle you ultimately want to live. Of course depending on your current and projected income, your lifestyle goals will vary. I don't want to shoot anyone's lifestyle dreams down from the get-go, however, what I'm saying is that it should be pretty obvious that if you're a school teacher and you absolutely love being a school teacher and plan to make money from this and this only for the rest of your income generating life, most likely buying a private jet is not going to be part of your financial lifestyle goals. Sorry, but if this isn't obvious to you, you might need a slap of reality! How do you envision your future? Is it somewhat similar to your current lifestyle, or drastically different? What do you want your day-to-day or year-to-year lifestyle to look like?

Let's start with some basics. I always knew I wanted the lifestyle, creativity, and tax benefits (of course) of having my own company. When I first started Black Hawk Financial, I had already lived and worked my butt off in the financial services sector all over the world including Toronto, Los Angeles, New York, Nice, Vancouver, Chicago, and London. After all of these incredible learning experiences I decided I didn't want anyone else to dictate when I had to wake up, go to sleep, arrive at, or leave the office again.

I'm probably busier now with the amount of business travel I do than I ever was while working for someone else.

In the intense world of global financial markets, the work hours and lifestyle I committed to were a huge sacrifice personally. It taught me how to be tough, how to network, how to go after what I want, and how to get through long days with little to no sleep after days on end of travel and living on plane food. I still try to keep up with the financial markets because investing and financial education are my true passions, but, again, now it's on my terms. Even now my life is often exhausting beyond comprehension, yet it's deeply fulfilling and so worth it.

My first vision of how I wanted my life to look was rather entrepreneurial and on a day-to-day lifestyle basis in terms of scheduling. This matches my strengths perfectly; anyone who knows me will tell you I'm a non-stop planner, organizer, and fill my travel and daily calendar up weeks or months in advance—year-round. Aside from fitting everything into my life, I also wanted to be able to have enough money that I never had to worry about paying the mortgage, rent, bills, having a nice car, vacations when I wanted (if my entrepreneur schedule allows), beautiful clothing, and so much more including many charitable ventures, and giving back to my community.

One thing I know and value more than any kind of financial tool is this: **spending time or money on yourself and your own wants pales in comparison to the joy and love you feel in your heart when you give to someone else in need.** As the Dalai Lama says, *"Living a meaningful life isn't just a matter of money. It's about dedicating your life to helping others."* He also says, *"If you think you are too small to make a difference, try sleeping with a mosquito."* Both quotes are fitting and equally important.

What Are Your Lifestyle Priorities?

Not the entrepreneurial type? That's okay! Not everyone

wants the pressure, hours, and responsibility of running a business and managing employees. Many of my friends don't want to own homes either, they'd rather travel five weeks a year and not have to worry about the responsibility of a home. You can prioritize whatever goals and lifestyle factors you want in your Financial Nirvana. If you know you're going to be limited with a certain salary/income range for most of your life or the foreseeable future (plus any money you make investing of course), it's all the more important for you to be in the right money mindset for allocating your income; this ensures you are making the absolute most of every dollar, so you can meet your lifestyle goals and live the dream. Once you actually think about and recognize your priorities, you can pinpoint what you need to live the way you want.

There's a lot you can accomplish in terms of lifestyle goals on any salary or income level, including becoming a millionaire on a teacher's wage at thirty-six, if that's your goal (check out the video on the YFF website). Use what you already have to your advantage (your money and your personal strengths) to put your goals into action. Once you start to create your list of lifestyle priorities, you will see that the list can be broken down between your basic **needs** and your many **wants**. This is your first piece of *good life work* for this chapter. Most people want to spend now for instant gratification, but that's the fast track to being broke.

Chapter Bonus:

Make a list of your personal **Lifestyle Needs vs. Wants** over the next 10 years by sequence of priority. Download this worksheet on the website. Filling this out will get you on your way to designing your dream life, which we'll talk about in the next chapter.

Identify Your Strengths: What's Going to Get You There?

Getting to your Financial Nirvana starts with believing in yourself and your strengths. To allow yourself to achieve your own dream lifestyle, you need to put your best foot forward, using the strengths you already have at your disposal to get you where you want to be. Not only does this include the field you're educated or experienced in, how much money you have in your bank account now, your network of mentors and influencers, but it also includes your personal strengths, for example, interpersonal skills, attention to detail, patience, and organizational skills. Your strengths include anything that comes easiest or most naturally to you.

When it comes to your financial future, your strengths often get mixed in with your interests and hobbies as well, as these could be great money making opportunities and should be considered when planning out your goals and dreams. Feel free to include these in your list of strengths I'm about to ask you to create. All of these items will be helpful for the next chapter where we combine your vision, strengths, weaknesses, needs, and wants to create your *Financial Nirvana Timeline*.

Chapter Bonus:

Head to the website to download the **Identify your Strengths worksheet;** this will set you up to dream big in Chapter 3.

Summary

In the last chapter we looked at what your weaknesses are when it comes to money and your personal spending and saving habits. You've also now had a chance to think about your personal strengths and passions, and all the needs and wants you have for your current and future financial life. Remember, it's often easy to be swayed by those promising the easy path to wealth and financial abundance. In some cases it might be easier than you think and you might need someone like me or another financial professional to show you the way; however, for the most part these schemes can be dangerous and get you into worse trouble with your finances than you already are. Beware!

Living financially well isn't about instant gratification; it's about building a sustainable, enjoyable, ideal life, and creating a life that strikes the perfect balance between all of your needs and wants. In the next chapter it all comes together to create your empowering and exciting *Financial Nirvana*.

My Two Cents:

- Stop wasting more of your time, money, and effort on get rich quick schemes.

- **Living in *Financial Nirvana* means making the absolute most of your money, allowing you to meet your lifestyle goals to live a fulfilling and abundant life.**

- Your priorities are your needs and wants; listing these in order of priority will help you see where you should be allocating your monthly/annual income.

- Identifying your personal strengths, areas of knowledge and experience, and interests and passions will help guide you to ways to make more money and create your own wealth.

Chapter Bonuses:

1) Make a list of your personal **Lifestyle Needs vs. Wants** for the next 10 years. Download this **worksheet** from the website. Filling this out will get you on your way to designing your dream life, which we'll talk about in the next chapter.

2) Head to the website to download the **Identify your Strengths worksheet**; this will set you up to dream big in Chapter 3!

Chapter 3

Get out of Your Own Way and Dream Big! Step 3 on your Path to Financial Nirvana

"Every day I get up and look through the Forbes list of the richest people in America. If I'm not there, I go to work."
~ Robert Orben

WE'RE GETTING THERE. YOU'VE now actively thought about your *needs* and *wants*, the key to being able to live your life free from money stress. You should be getting excited by the fact that you can be debt-free, live comfortably, have time flexibility, and be stress-free. If you're being even somewhat realistic about the wants on your list (i.e. you're not planning to live on a minimum wage income for the rest of your life, or you want to charter a private jet for year round vacations), you can and will make it happen.

This chapter is specifically structured to show you how to have the right money mindset, how to truly believe in yourself, and how to take action with the proper plan and tools in place. The *good life work* in the previous chapter is super important here so get yours ready.

You will also learn **The Two Most Important Things Your Money Should Provide You.** *Hint:* It's not ego and a social media following, although it could do that too.

Step 3 in Creating Your Financial Nirvana is all about determining your true values and priorities in order to dream big and get what you really want out of life.

Get Down to Business: What and Who Will Need Your Money in the Next Ten Years?

Let's get back to what living financially free and what freedom in general means to you. The beauty about all of this is that it's your money and your life. Meaning, you can do whatever your heart desires with your hard earned cash; unfortunately, going straight to the *wants* list and using your cash for instant gratification is often what lands people *in the red* with their accounts—credit, debt, and not being able to take care of basic needs.

In the last chapter, I asked you to create your lists of wants and needs in sequence of priority. Your needs and required expenses must be the base of your financial life plan. Yes, we will incorporate all of the fun lifestyle and discretionary spending items as well, but the first thing to know is what your true cost of living is on a month-to-month, annual, and potential five to ten year basis.

The most important thing to know about being in the right money mindset is that your money should provide you with two things: confidence and security. What are the biggest priorities and needs you have as far as money goes? Your monthly and annual needs might include things such as caring for yourself and your family's basic needs—housing, transportation, food, committed debts, education, clothing, medical and other insurance, health and wellness. Your five- to ten-year priorities might have these same needs, with some additional allocations toward covering the expenses of a spouse, children, or an elderly parent.

It might seem strange to start planning out your family and children before you have them, but the purpose of this exercise is to envision what your life will or might possibly look like in the future and how you need to lay the foundation for that future now. There is no time to waste. No matter what stage you're at, having a plan that considers your future responsibilities and requirements for your money is something you need to plan for today.

Do you have aging parents or family members that might require your assistance for their living or medical needs? Do your parents have enough money to cover their retirement and in-home care should they require it? If not, you may want to add this to your list as they too might have to rely on you and your income in the future, which is something you may not have thought of while creating your needs and wants lists for your financial future.

Why Plan for Ten Years?

You may be thinking, if you're going to look ten years into the future now, why not look twenty or thirty years ahead? While retirement should absolutely be considered, particularly if you're over forty, this book is structured to give you a realistic look at your current situation and how to take the first steps toward independence.

For many people, basic needs and wants aren't being met right now. Making a financial plan is something that will need to be shifted and adjusted as life changes. Your job/income won't always stay the same, your priorities change, schedules change, and so does everything else.

Let's start planning your financial future from where you are now. The great thing is, you can easily use the same tools and processes of analysis and planning to adjust your plan for the future as well. You merely need to revisit your plan, priorities, and desires when you go through a major change.

Keep this in mind if you are getting married or expecting children soon.

We'll All Be Gray One Day

What's said in this book about looking ahead ten years is in no way to diminish the effect retirement planning should have on your overall financial goals. It's so important to understand the power that compounding interest and investing has within your 401(k), IRA, Roth IRA (USA), RRSP, TFSA (Canada) and other registered retirement savings plans (more on this in Chapter 7). Having access to this money at a reduced or zero tax rate when you retire is why you must take advantage of employer offered retirement contribution programs. Always make sure you're making the maximum amount of contributions to your retirement fund up to the amount your employer is willing to match. Many companies match your contributions up to 6 percent of your salary (this is **free money**). Ask human resources where you work if you're eligible for this or other benefits.

Let's take a look at a very simplistic example of the costs of retirement. Take your basic costs like mortgage/rent, food, transportation, medical, insurance, and clothing expenses every month, and multiply it by twelve months. For example, $3,500 per month would be $42,000 for the year. Now, how many years do you wish to enjoy retirement? Thirty years? If so, 30 years x $42,000 = $1.26M. This will show you approximately how much money you'll need to live your current lifestyle during retirement (excluding inflation and an increase in expected medical expenses that may not be covered by your health insurance – something we'll discuss further in Chapter 9).

Again, this vision of your retired life might change over the course of time as your financial situation improves over the next ten years, particularly if you follow the strategies outlined in this book. There are a lot of amazing free online calculators where you can play around with your own numbers to show you how the earlier you start taking advantage of the beauty of compounding interest in your retirement funds, the easier saving for retirement or any other long term financial goal will be.

I also find that planning for more than ten years in advance is often a waste of time depending on your age and expected changes in your lifestyle. Not to say that it isn't a healthy exercise to go through what your required cash flow, income, investments, needs, and wants might be beyond ten years or when you're retired, but creating detailed plans or timelines for much more than ten years in the future is unrealistic unless you plan on your life being static, and it won't be. You also shouldn't want it to be. I hope for my own sake and for those reading this book that so many incredible life changes and opportunities will come our way, that our financial and personal lives will be light-years ahead from where they are now in ten or more years. Cheers to a future of health, wealth, happiness, and wisdom.

The Fun Stuff! Live Financially Free on Your Own Terms—Your Wants

We've covered what your thought process should be when prioritizing and analyzing your basic needs and expenses. Now, what do you really want? This includes everything from material items to lifestyle goals and attributes. What does your dream lifestyle look like? How many hours a week do you work? Do you vacation? Do you own a home? Multiple homes? Fancy cars? Get your nails done every week? Attend sporting events and concerts? Go boating on the weekends? Buy your parents a home? What about starting a foundation and making a difference in the world? None of these things are absolute needs, but they sure do make life enjoyable. Whatever is on your list, I hope it excites you to think that having them is possible.

My own personal wants list started with two things:

i)   To not be tied to someone else's schedule and efficiency parameters (i.e. *working smarter not harder*).

ii) To leave a legacy.

In the previous section I mentioned the two most important things your money should provide you:

i)   Confidence

ii) Security

I want to be able to pass along to you, and everyone I can possibly spread the word to, that you don't have to be rich to live a secure, abundant, debt-free, mostly stress-free life. In no way is it going to be perfect all the time, but being able to travel the world on my own dime, enjoy as much time as I want with my family and friends, and be the one to decide what I'm going to do with my day-to-day life—while sharing my passion for financial literacy and empowering others to do the same—is my dream life. I'm already here, and I'm constantly adding more needs and wants to my lists as life changes, but this was the foundation of my own wants:

1) **Entrepreneurship:** Make my own career and schedule as I see fit for me. To be fulfilled by my daily work and lifestyle. Being an entrepreneur allows me to multitask and be highly efficient all day long—something I wasn't getting working full-time for other companies.

2) **Leave a legacy:** To share my passion with other people by showing them how to meet their financial and lifestyle goals—no matter where they are now. I know that you don't have to be a financial genius or a

math whiz to be smart with your money and allow it to help you reach your dreams.

Back to your needs and wants. From the lists you created in your *good life work* last chapter, look at this list again and determine your top five, then write a goal date next to each one. Yes these can be adjusted, but it is always good to start with a goal date to remind you what you're truly working toward when you have to make tough calls about your spending and money decisions. (Did I forget to mention that the road to financial freedom isn't always easy?) There will be decisions to be made.

Unless you magically start making a lot more money next week or next month, you need to start your financial plan from where you are right now. There is no better day than today so let's keep going. Think about your needs and wants; post the lists on your fridge, or on Post-it notes on your bathroom mirror. Or you could create an image of them and make it your wallpaper on your computer and phone. Use visual reminders of what you're working toward and all the great things that will come your way if you do the work necessary to overcome any financial challenges you may currently be experiencing.

> *"The best way to predict your future is to create it."*
> ~ Abraham Lincoln

The Dream Big Ten-Year Timeline: Your Needs and Wants

There is a trick to the art of putting together all your needs and wants into actual commitments you can stick to in order to reach your own ultimate Financial Nirvana. This will show you how to put all your needs and wants into the same place, on the same timeline, to determine where your needs will intersect with your wants and how to envision and plan ahead for the times when additional funds will be required. It should also excite you for what's ahead. You need to build a framework in order to gain clarity and set the intention for your life moving forward. It will also be helpful in showing you what types of returns you will need to achieve from your investments in order to meet these goals.

Putting pen to paper with exercises like this will give you the confidence in knowing that you can achieve most (or all) of your needs and wants, and you will get there by implementing the right plan with the right tools. It's also important to note that this timeline exercise should be done alongside your spouse or significant other so you have complete transparency in the relationship, ensuring your values and plans are aligned. If you're single, consider finding an accountability partner whose judgment you trust that you can voice your plans and concerns to. This person should act as a support to you and shouldn't be afraid to call you out when they see you starting to veer off course.

Chapter Bonus:

To get you started I've created a Financial Nirvana Timeline exercise; this is your Chapter 3 *good life work.* Doing this exercise might take some time, as you really need to consider your lists of needs and wants, and your overall values in both priority and time order. To make sure you're focused on this most important exercise without distraction, I suggest that you and your spouse or accountability partner set aside a personal finance day, or even a few of hours with no distractions, to construct, review, and consider your choices. Give each other enough time to think of any potential roadblocks that might come up along the way and how to plan for these in your timeline.

Want More Money? Unleash Your Untapped Potential—Create a $ide Hustle

It doesn't grow on trees so it's time to get serious! It might be a little scary to think of all the financial goals and milestones you've set out for yourself. Fair enough. It's not called Nirvana or the dream life for nothing. A great way to make your wants and needs much more easily attainable is to think of your assets and strengths, and how you can use these, together with your experience, to create additional income. What do I mean by a side hustle? Doing something that interests you, that you're passionate about, or that you are really good at for extra money. Some examples of side hustles might be tutoring, social media management, babysitting, animal boarding or walking, affiliate marketing, landscaping, podcasting, blogging, design consulting, repairing cars, helping people build their Ikea furniture and other odd jobs around the house, tax prep, housesitting, background acting, and the list goes on. There are so many things that small businesses and individuals need help with and you can easily create a side job or even a full-time business by providing a quality service at a price that matches or beats other providers in your area.

Aside from your personal skills, putting your underutilized assets, like your car, to work on a website like Turo.com may be an option for you. This website allows you to list your car for rent when you're not using it. You can do the same with your camera or other equipment. Craigslist, Monster, Kijiji, Angie's List, Fiverr, and Upwork are all great places where you can post and advertise your side hustle. Always make sure you ask your satisfied clients to provide you with references, testimonials, and Google or other site reviews to help boost your brand and revenues. Who knows, one of these odd jobs could turn into the entrepreneurial venture you've always wanted? Or, allow you to take that extra vacation you just wrote about in your Financial Nirvana timeline!

What's Your Money Mindset?

I can't say it enough, being in the right money mindset is the single most important aspect of being able to reach your financial goals. You need to believe in yourself to accomplish anything in life. Now that you know what, why, and when, you can determine *how* by taking action.

Summary

We have explored the real guts of why and what you need to fulfill your own Financial Nirvana. Most importantly, I outlined the money mindset you need to have when approaching these ambitious goals. How are you going to get there? We thought about this piece a little bit here in Chapter 3, exploring different ideas for a side hustle business, however, there is so much more to take action on than simply looking for ways to make more money. It's what you do with the money you have that will determine whether you succeed or fail in your financial life.

The fourth step toward living the dream is taking action. Over the next five chapters, we'll discuss and learn about spending, saving, paying off debt, and making the most of your credit score and credit cards - don't shudder, they can be a wonderful financial tool. Try not to be overwhelmed; simply take it at your own pace. One page at a time.

My Two Cents:

- Using your cash to satisfy your *wants* for instant gratification is what often lands people **in the red** in the first place.

- The most important thing to know about being in the right *money mindset* is that **your money should provide you with two things: confidence and security.**

- When first planning your Financial Nirvana, try a **ten-year outlook** as this type of plan is something that will need to be adjusted as life shifts; anything beyond ten years from now isn't as relevant to your current situation.

- Create a timeline of your ten-year *wants* and *needs* to see how they intersect and where you biggest areas of financial need are.

- Unleash your untapped potential; create a **side hustle** and **make money** from your passions.

- Having the right money mindset is the single most important aspect of being able to reach your financial goals.

CHAPTER BONUS:

To get you started, I've created a **Financial Nirvana Timeline exercise** for you; check it out at **www. youngfunfree.com**

Chapter 4

Hey Big Spender - Take Action! Step 4 on your Path to Financial Nirvana

"The safest way to double your money is to fold it over and put it in your pocket."
~ Kin Hubbard

YOU NOW KNOW WHAT direction you're headed in, and I hope you're excited for the fulfilling life you have ahead. No matter where you're starting from, with the right tools and actions, you will get there. *Action* is the key word. We've learned all about steps one through three on your *Path to Financial Nirvana;* now onto *Step 4—Taking Action.* There are many areas of your financial life where you can and must take action, which will be explored over the coming chapters. The first is the most important when starting from square one—the basics of financial management—spending: ***how to live within your means.*** Do you spend less than you make? What habits do you have when it comes to spending your money? Is your money providing you the security and confidence you need and deserve? Are you spending wisely on both your primal needs and lifestyle wants? Or are insecurities and instant gratification getting in the way?

It can be daunting to talk about all the money you've been spending (unwisely for many I'm sure), but it truly is the first step in taking action. Do you really need all the things you're paying for? The tools and strategies in this book aren't focused on sacrifice and deprivation, but about finding solutions and a better way to live. Is there a way you can get what you want for less? By finding the things you need and want for a better price, your financial future will be much brighter and your dreams will actually be attainable. Live the high life at a better price and build your wealth in the meantime. Let's dive in.

What's Your Spending Power?

Probably the biggest issue I see with most clients, friends, and family members looking for financial guidance is that they believe that in order achieve their goals they need to make more money; they don't think enough about how they're spending the money they already have. **Your true spending power is your net income after taxes and other expenses incurred to generate income**. Given that you should be thinking about your spending and budget guidelines in terms of your actual spending power and net income, you may not have as much to spend as you thought. Have you been living within your real means? The truth for many is that you've probably been living and spending without actually thinking of these things, hoping to end up with a positive account balance at the end of the month.

Did you know that according to a 2017 Pricewaterhouse-Coopers survey, *"70 percent of Millennials consistently carry balances on their credit cards and 45 percent use their credit cards for monthly expenses they could not afford otherwise"*? This has a great impact on your long-term financial goals. Depending on your goals, you should definitely be asking for the raise you deserve, or you might need to start a side hustle, change your housing situation, or move on to a better paying job. However, for the most part, you would probably be able to reach your goals by simply being smarter with the money you already earn.

It is much easier to cut your expenses than to earn more income. Start here.

Crisis Mode! Are You There yet?

Two major factors that hold people back when looking at how they use their money to provide them with confidence and security are:

1) Insecurities and keeping up with the Joneses

2) Instant gratification—I want it now! This will make me happy now = impulse, unconscious spending

"We want everything so fast that we're the ones becoming slower. Slower mentally, physically, emotionally, spiritually."
~ Pitbull, The Tony Robbins Podcast

As we've discussed previously, the inner need many people have in our online culture of comparison is to keep up with our peers, the Joneses, in terms of the lifestyles they live and material items they have. The need for immediate satisfaction from impulse purchases, like a round of drinks for everyone at the bar, or that perfect dress to wear to the party tonight, is the culture that keeps many people's debt and paycheck-to-paycheck living spiraling out of control. Being broke after every paycheck is unnecessary stress and suffering. What these spending patterns really come down to is **unconscious spending**.

The best part is you don't need a lot of money to be financially secure. You will be more fulfilled, healthy, and less stressed in your day-to-day life when you use the money you have to the best of your ability, stretching it as far as it will go by making wise, conscience purchases and scoring great deals on the items on your *needs* list first; purchasing items on your *wants* list second.

I've had many friends and colleagues with instant gratification spending behaviors complain to me that they have no money in their bank accounts; they blow through every paycheck faster than they earn it. The sad thing is they don't even realize what they're doing wrong. Again, the prime reason for me to write this book. If you find yourself asking this same question every time you look at your account balances, please pay attention.

The Path Too Often Taken—Time to Smarten Up!

By now many of you may already realize that you have a major spending problem. It could be a self-control and unconscious spending issue, or you believe you simply have too many expenses on your needs list to support your current lifestyle, and you can't meet these needs every month. Either way, the financial crisis you're headed for if you stay on the same path is dire, and no one wants this for you. No one wants to see someone they love struggling to get by, with the stress of money weighing you down and preventing you from getting ahead and enjoying life. With a bit of analysis of your spending patterns, and by getting into the right money mindset, we can pinpoint where you're going wrong and how to fix it.

It's annoying but true—the most overused cliché of all time: *"The definition of insanity is doing the same thing over and over again and expecting different results." ~ Albert Einstein*

OR

As I might say: *The definition of insanity is making the exact same mistakes over and over again, expecting shit to change. That. Is. Crazy!*

Figure Out Where You Are Now

1. What's the Current Situation?

Pull out your *good life work* from Chapter 2 and let's take a look at your *needs* and *wants* lists. I want you to put a checkmark on your lists next to every need or want that you're already meeting with your current approach to spending. If you generally pay your rent and other mandatory bills like utilities, insurance, school, and transportation on time, have a few dinners out with friends each month, and are able to take a vacation once a year, put a checkmark next to these items on the lists, and others that apply.

Keep in mind these are items on your lists that you actually pay for every month/year and they are paid off in full without accumulating debt. By this I mean whether you pay for these items using cash, pre-approved debit transactions, e-transfers, or credit card (without accumulating a revolving balance), you're in the black.

Haven't heard this term before? In the finance world *in the black* is when a company produces positive earnings after accounting for all of its expenses, often a hallelujah! moment of celebration for many companies. The term is also used as it applies to personal finance when people are struggling to get out of debt to become cash flow positive or have their accounts in the black.

2. What if I'm Doing Okay with My Needs and Wants Now, but I Still Have Debt Looming Over Me?

If you're holding onto credit card or other bad debts from past mistakes, you're still *in the red* (i.e. still at a net loss/ unprofitable/in debt). I mentioned the red zone in the last chapter, and it's a scary place to be, as anyone will know who's ever not paid their credit card balance on time, in full, and seen the interest amounts.

Although, depending on your age, learning some tough lessons when you're young can be a great thing. Generally, as we age, our lists of needs and responsibilities often get longer and longer, with more people to take care of who count on us for emotional and financial support. Learning the tough lessons of how and when to spend, and how to get out of debt can be a real asset in the future. We'll talk more about **getting back to black** in Chapter 8.

3. Needs and Wants—What Needs and Wants You Aren't Meeting

Keep those lists in front of you. Look at them again and see the items on your lists that aren't checked off. By cross-referencing the lists you created in Chapter 2 with the Financial Nirvana Timeline from Chapter 3, you will start to see where there are holes in your plan. Transfer the checkmarks from your lists onto your timeline and see what's missing—in the next two years even. Now, how much would it cost you per year to attain those needs and wants annually? Do you currently have enough money left in your bank accounts for the next two years to acquire these items or meet these lifestyle goals? Or are you barely making it by with what you already spend your money on? This leads me to my next topic.

It Ain't the Daily Latte . . . It's ALL Your Spending Habits!

It takes a lot more than stopping your Starbucks habit to live the dream. It drives me crazy listening to financial experts and others speak about cutting back on your latte habit and other crazy ideas to get you to financial freedom. I'll tell you something right now: it takes a hell of a lot more than changing your caffeine preferences to get to nirvana. Your overall spending habits are what got you in your current situation, not the fact that you enjoy Starbucks daily, although that is one thing you could change to improve your overall financial status. Every little bit adds up. Calculate how much your takeout coffee habit costs you annually and make the decision whether it's worth it or not (see below).

Is Your Spending out of Whack with Your True Priorities?

Now that you've taken a look at how close you are to attaining everything on your needs and wants lists, you need to look at your current spending patterns and categories, maybe where you're spending too much money. Is your spending aligned with your priorities? This is where we can start to determine how to make the biggest impact on your budget.

American households spend the largest portion of their income on housing, 35 percent on average. Of course, depending on the size and location of your family, your spending in different categories will vary. For example, while living and working in cities like Vancouver, London, Toronto, and Nice the cost of housing is so high that for many people this figure may be closer to 50 percent of your monthly or annual budget. In that case, I'd suggest looking at some other options to get that amount down; although if living in your own apartment or house in a bustling urban center is high on your list of priorities, then perhaps you'll have to sacrifice more heavily in other areas to make it happen (or get a side hustle going for extra income).

There are many types of great free tools that banks and credit card companies have created to allow clients to analyze their monthly and annual spending. My American Express online statement breaks down all my spending into categories so I can see where I'm spending most of my money (travel and entertainment). You might have this automated for your accounts as well. Play around with your online banking or ask your local branch for more information about tools that are available to you.

Are you spending more in one area of your life than another? Is this aligned with your needs and wants? How do you know? Don't fool yourself into thinking it's okay to skip this step. Seeing your true situation for what it is will be an eye-opener and it's important in taking the first step toward action and getting **real results.** To make sure you do this step the right way, I'm offering a **free consultation** to those who want to be guided through the process. Set yourself up for success. Go to **www.youngfunfree.com** for more information.

What Do I Do Now? Think Preservation, Not Deprivation

Only you can decide if your financial independence is important enough to change your ways. By analyzing your spending patterns to find your biggest sources of financial weakness, you can determine where your spending is misaligned with your true priorities. From this, you can take action by putting your money back where it truly belongs.

By making wise decisions that are aligned with your overall lifestyle goals, you will get to where you want to be.

Want to go on vacation for three weeks every year? If you moved from a one-bedroom apartment to a studio, would you be able to save enough money to go on that three-week vacation? Which is more of a priority? Or maybe you could take transit to work instead of car payments, insurance, and parking? These are simplistic examples to illustrate that life is about choices, give and take. Depending on your income, some of the things on your wants list may be out of reach at the moment. However, there are many ways you can be much more effective with your current income if you put thought into your daily money choices. Below is a simple budget guideline to get you started on determining whether your spending is falling in line with the typical standards.

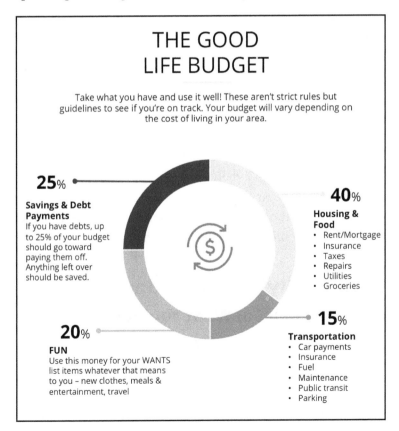

THE GOOD LIFE BUDGET

Take what you have and use it well! These aren't strict rules but guidelines to see if you're on track. Your budget will vary depending on the cost of living in your area.

25%

Savings & Debt Payments
If you have debts, up to 25% of your budget should go toward paying them off. Anything left over should be saved.

40%

Housing & Food
- Rent/Mortgage
- Insurance
- Taxes
- Repairs
- Utilities
- Groceries

20%

FUN
Use this money for your WANTS list items whatever that means to you – new clothes, meals & entertainment, travel

15%

Transportation
- Car payments
- Insurance
- Fuel
- Maintenance
- Public transit
- Parking

Spend Well, Live Well Strategies

Learning to stretch your money as far as it will go is the only way to achieve as many things on your needs and wants lists as possible. I exercise and eat well (almost) every day to ensure my body and mind are working at optimal capacity; the same theory applies to financial wellness—I am frugal with my spending and implement my own tools to know I will get optimal results and stretch with my money. Setting yourself up for financial success starts with knowing how to use your money in the most efficient ways. In order to achieve everything on your needs and wants lists, you have to be focused on the outcome, prepared for some level of sacrifice and hard work, and make the most of what you have.

I use many strategies to stretch my money to the best of my ability every single day in order to meet my basic life needs and lots of my wants and luxuries as well. Making small changes to give you financial comfort and added room in your discretionary spending budget or savings pool is an ongoing process that should be applied daily.

Here are ten ideas you should be considering in your everyday life to make your dreams attainable. I use each and every one of these on a daily basis and they make a world of difference in how far my money goes. Remember: preservation not deprivation. Enjoy your money and all the fun and comforts it can provide by spending smartly.

Ten Frugality Tools - Spend and Save!
Make the Most of What You Have

(This list is also available in PDF on the website.)

1) **Comparison Shopping:** Online vs. Offline prices, service guarantees, and warranties; look online at the many comparison shopping websites, tools, and coupons apps available.

2) **Rewards Programs:** Collect points and rewards to use toward travel and transportation (air, hotels, meals, gas), free upgrades, and other items you would normally be paying for anyways. (See Chapter 5 on credit cards.)

3) **Car Leases:** Do lease takeovers at discounted rates through people needing to get out of their lease agreements early. I use a website called www.lease-busters.com or Craigslist for this; I'm sure there are many others as well. This is a great way to get nice, nearly new cars still under warranty at amazing discounts. Many people put cash down when they start a lease to decrease the monthly payment amounts; this is to your advantage and unfortunately their loss when you take over the lease. For example, I took over the lease on a fancy new car, and over the next thirty-six months of the lease I will have saved $9000 compared to what the car would have cost me if I leased it new right off the lot myself. A lot of people who need to move quickly or are eager to get rid of their vehicles will even offer cash incentives for you to take over their lease (mine was $900). This is done with all kinds of vehicles; check out the sites above.

4) **Meals & Groceries:** Always look for sales and markdowns on the most expensive items on your grocery list like meats and seafood (proteins). Stock up on these marked down items and freeze them. You can use these for up to six months generally. Also check out organic pantry items on sale at stores like Whole Foods, Trader Joes, and the natural sections of other supermarkets. They have amazing deals on staples every week. You don't have to sacrifice your health or food standards to live frugally.

Another big idea—pack your lunch. There are *no free*

lunches as they say, and spending $15/day on lunch is approximately $3,960/year. Could you go on vacation for that instead? How about investing it in an Index Fund and earning 7% interest that compounds?

Have you considered the additional health benefits from cooking your own food instead of grabbing takeout? Small changes can make a big difference to your body and wallet. Groceries are a family's biggest expense outside of transportation and housing, yet this is where many people waste the most amount of money and don't even think about it. Plan your meals according to what's on sale and in season, use generic pantry products (most of these products use the same manufacturer as the brand name products anyway). Remember, these are after tax, net income dollars that you're spending. Even more reason to be frugal at the supermarket.

5) **Health and Fitness: Healthy body, healthy wallet!** Most of the monetarily measured wealthy and successful people I know are also aware of their physical well-being. It's no accident that I, and other entrepreneurs and financially well people, stick to diligent exercise, mindfulness, and healthy eating routines. There is an absolute correlation between having a healthy mind, body, and wallet. Keeping up with my daily workouts provides me with the endorphins I need to keep stress at bay, while helping me stay sharp, engaged, and energized through long days. Try using some of the tools here to keep yourself and your bank account fit.

There are some super easy ways to save money and enjoy the social and physical benefits of exercise. Almost every gym, boutique studio, recreation or fitness center offers free first visits, or trials for anywhere from one week to three months at deeply discounted rates. I've been a longtime member of ClassPass; this is a membership service that allows you to attend group classes at almost any gym or boutique studio in most major cities all over North America, Europe, the United Kingdom, and Australia. I use my $90/month (CAD) ClassPass membership to go to classes like Body by Simone, Barry's Bootcamp and other celebrity workout studios that have typical drop-in rates of $35+ (USD) per class. It's a great deal and a fun way to keep your mind and body stimulated through fun, high quality, trendy workouts that you can switch up whenever you like. Most yoga studios, recreation/community centers, Lululemon stores, RYU (Respect Your Universe), and other apparel stores offer free or donation-based karma and community classes weekly or even daily. Search online for these discounted and free classes in your area. You can also look for new gym deals on Groupon, LivingSocial, and other e-commerce marketplaces.

6) **The Daily Latte:** Yes, I do save money on my daily caffeine habit. I like to make my own in the morning with a nice machine (or even instant, I'm not too particular), although there are so many amazing machines for home use ranging in quality and price per cup. That said, I am still a Starbucks Gold Member and proud of it. Again, if you're at a place in life where you're meeting all or most of the needs and wants on your lists while saving toward your goals adequately, feel free to spend your extra discretionary money as you wish.

7) **Free Shipping:** For those of you who don't already order at least the minimum amount on Amazon

for free shipping, or have Amazon Prime, buy other items on your overall household shopping list to get free shipping. If you're on any other site online, you can often find free shipping codes by doing a Google search or adding a coupon finder to your browser.

8) **Email Subscriber Promotions:** Over 70% of email marketing offers use free shipping, free trials, and other discounts to entice you to subscribe to their websites. Take the offer. You can always unsubscribe from the emails later if the company is clogging up your inbox.

9) **Craigslist, Kijiji, and the Free sections:** I can't even tell you how many iPhones, furniture pieces, concert tickets, and other items my friends, family, and I have bought on Craigslist. I once bought a like new custom leather sofa worth thousands of dollars for 85% off the retail price. When investing in real estate rentals, this is a huge asset to be able to redesign and furnish homes and offices stylishly and affordably.

Family Story: My brother's personal favorite (yes, money sense runs in the family) is the Craigslist Free section. My brother has acquired more appliances, electronics, sport bikes, scooters, ATVs, cars, trailers, sports equipment, and other toys than I can even count. It's a goldmine for those who know how to use it. He has apps on his phone and browser that notify him when certain high-ticket items are posted in the Free section so he can jump on them as soon as they go live. His typical side hustle income from buying, restoring, and selling one to two items is roughly $1000/month. Not bad for a few hours work. He once spent months saving up for a hot tub he wanted, only to have the exact same one show up on the Craigslist free section. It works perfectly and he still has it two years later. If you've never checked out this section, it's a must. (Hint: side hustle opportunity!)

10) **Renegotiating your phone, internet, and cable bills:** We all know that phone companies often give promotions to new customers for the first six months or year to draw them into a new contract. Are you sure you're getting the best price for your mobile and home services? Call your provider and ask if they have any current promotions, or if they'd be willing to match other provider's rates. Get a discount to bundle all your services into one company. I guarantee you'll see some savings.

Summary

When it comes to your spending habits and making your money work better for you, change takes good advice, diligence, and action. The suggestions in this chapter are relatively simple; however, the key to making these strategies work for you and getting the most from your income is putting them into action. You can save anywhere between 15-90% off retail prices using the frugal strategies and ideas in this chapter. If you get smart about your money now, it will save you a world of pain in the future and allow you to thoroughly enjoy the time and money you have. Life shouldn't be about restriction, but in some cases you should restrict yourself from spending too much on items you know you don't truly value. Life should be exciting. Be excited that you're getting started on the path to your newfound financial wellness! Ever heard of short-term pain for long-term gain? Prime example right here.

As I've said before, impulse spending is your fast track to broke, leaving you unable to have the other things you truly want in your life. Next time your friends ask you to go out for dinner and drinks, invite everyone over to your place instead and create your own supper club. Playing hostess can be fun and save you a lot of money. With each and every step you take toward having your true financial priorities in order, your money mindset will improve and you'll be able to see that the small sacrifices are worth it.

My Two Cents:

- The biggest issue I see with most clients, friends, and family looking for financial guidance is that they believe that in order achieve their goals they need to make more money and don't consider how they're spending the money they have now.

- It is much easier to cut back your expenses than to earn more income, start here.

- **Three major issues that hold people back** from getting ahead when it comes to their spending:

  1) **Insecurities: Keeping up with the Joneses.**

  2) **Instant Gratification: I want it now! Unconscious spending.**

  3) **I can't keep up: Feeling overwhelmed by your "needs" without the income to cover it.**

- **Get your priorities straight.** Figure out where you're overspending to see how you can make room for higher priorities.

- Learn how to **stretch your money as far as it will go** in order to achieve as many things on your needs and wants lists as possible; it's the only way to get where you want to be.

- Get your **free consultation!** Let me walk you through your own personal spending and situational analysis. **Visit www.youngfunfree.com to sign up!**

- Baby Steps: Use the **Ten Frugality Tools** to enhance your life and stretch your dollars.

Chapter Bonuses:

1) Ten Frugal Tools online PDF.

2) **I'm offering a FREE CONSULTATION to those who want to be walked through their own personal spending and situational analysis. Visit the website to sign up.**

Chapter 5

The Credit Card Trap: The Pluses and Minuses of Credit Cards and Other Modes of Spending

"Money's only something you need in case you don't die tomorrow."
~ Carl Fox (Martin Sheen) *Wall Street*

IN THE LAST CHAPTER we discussed how while making more money is great, using the money you're earning now more wisely will get you well on your way to accomplishing the items on your needs and wants lists. By applying the right spending tools and strategies, you will have the basic skills required to live the life of your dreams. How well you implement these skills is the primary factor in determining your financial future.

Rather than talking about your saving habits next, I want to discuss the ways in which you spend. The actual modes you use to spend money can have a drastic effect on your financial wellness, especially if you use credit cards. Different modes of spending include credit cards, pre-paid or secured credit cards, debit cards, cash, lines of credit, any way you have available to you to spend your money (or somebody else's). Depending on your personal situation and habits, there may be ways that are smarter than others to spend your money.

Smart People Doing Stupid Things

As I've said previously, one of the primary reasons why I wanted to write this book is that in all my travels and experiences in the finance world, as well as more creative fields like acting and modeling, I've met many highly intelligent people who make poor decisions with the way they spend and manage their money. I wanted to create more resources for people outside the finance world to be able to learn about the basic and best ways to manage their money.

A perfect example that illustrates how much money you make is not as important as what you do with it, is looking at the dismal financial results of professional athletes and lottery winners. We've all heard the cautionary tales of how 70 percent of people who get a big windfall or win a lottery end up broke in a few years or less (according to the National Endowment for Financial Education). The same goes for 78 percent of National Football League (NFL) players within two years of retirement, and an estimated 60 percent of National Basketball Association (NBA) players within five years of playing their last game, according to a 2009 Sports Illustrated article. These people didn't lose all of their money because they weren't paid enough or were stupid. They might be highly intelligent in other areas, but they may not have had an interest in learning how to manage money. When they came into a whole lot of it, they weren't able to manage, invest, and spend it wisely, which prevented them from growing their money and providing for their families for years to come. The exact same thing goes for average earners with families and budgets. If you don't know the ins and outs of basic financial concepts—like how credit, interest, compounding interest, taxes, and banking fees work—it's difficult to get a hold of your own situation before it spirals out of control.

This brings me to my next subject: the big D - debt. That dreadful, knotted, sick feeling in your stomach. It keeps you up at night and hinders your ability to enjoy life. First off, if you have debt in the way of student loans, credit cards, lines of credit, or anything else, don't worry. Most people carry some form of debt, especially homeowners with a mortgage. A 2015 report by the Pew Charitable Trusts, which examined debt through the generations, found that eight in ten Americans are indebted in some way, most often because of mortgages. This debt wasn't limited to young people getting started in life, but this increasingly applies to older generations as well. With that being said, there's a difference between good debt and bad debt.

If you currently have **bad debts (i.e. anything that decreases in value the minute you buy it, and/or doesn't increase your net worth or income)** like payday loans, unpaid credit cards, medical bills, car loans, and gambling debts, that's okay! Did I just say bad debts are okay? Yep. We all have to start from somewhere. In 2017, data collected from the U.S. Census Bureau and the Federal Reserve stated that 38.1 percent of American households carry credit card debt. The average credit card debt amount for balance-carrying households in 2016 was $16,048 USD (that's over ~$20,000 CAD).

So many people I speak with feel shameful for being in their current debt situation. Everyone has a story of how and why they got into debt—some stories more emotionally painful than others. For many, I can completely relate to how they got to where they are and sympathize with their situation. It wasn't because they are unintelligent people, they simply didn't know any better or ran out of other options. In order to find your way out of debt, you need to analyze how you got into debt in the first place.

Are You Spending Stupidly?
Understanding How Credit Cards Work

Let me start with this: You are not stupid, but your methods of spending might be. The good news is that making changes is fairly simple once you know better. Most people instinctively know that the proper way to spend their money is to earn it first and spend later, not spend first then pay for it eventually. That doesn't always happen, or the multi-trillion dollar credit card industry wouldn't exist. Have you been spending without fully realizing the consequences of not paying off those purchases fully, on time, every month when the balance of your credit card statement is due? We will take a look at what a month of purchases might cost you in the long run later in this chapter.

What Is a Credit Card?

A credit card allows you to borrow money from your bank (or another credit issuing financial institution like a credit union, or a retail shop like a department store with their own financial department), to make purchases in advance of paying for them. As long as you pay the issuer back within the grace period, usually fifteen to thirty days, you don't have to pay them any extra money (interest), only the amount of the purchases. Essentially, this is an interest-free short-term loan. However, if you don't pay the entire amount owing until even one day after the grace period, you will owe them for the cost of your purchases plus **interest** (a percentage of the amount you owe the issuer/credit card company for your unpaid balance). The interest amount owing will be in addition to what you owe them for the cost of your actual purchases. Got it? These interest amounts can be calculated daily or monthly and that's where the bills really start to add up.

I mentioned that I've had the opportunity to meet many highly intelligent people throughout my career who had no knowledge of basic financial concepts. A perfect example of this was in an interview I did with a SpaceX employee at a finance conference in Vegas this year. While this extremely intelligent young man knew everything you could imagine about rockets and other things I have no knowledge of, he really wished someone had taught him more about basic financial literacy concepts like how credit cards work. It's incredible how someone whose IQ is through the roof and who is one of the brightest people I've ever met doesn't know how credit cards and interest works.

Credit Cards and Interest Rates: What Is My Credit Card Debt Really Costing Me?

The interest rates on credit cards vary, usually between 15 to 29%, although there are rates outside of these parameters (I've seen up to 79.9%) depending on the card issuer and your personal credit score. Usually, banks and credit unions have lower interest rates, whereas retail store cards often carry higher rates and have a lower level of credit qualifications. The rate usually marketed to the consumer is the **annual percentage rate or APR**. Although this number is expressed in annual terms, it is usually used to calculate your interest owing for shorter periods of time like days and months. That said, if you're using your credit cards the right way by paying the balance in full every month you don't have to worry about the APR at all.

Note: If you don't pay your entire balance on time, credit card companies will charge you daily or monthly **compounded interest**. That means every single day you don't pay off your statement balance in full, your debt will grow as the amount of interest owing compounds.

Example: Let's say one month you decided to splurge and go on a weekend ski trip with some friends that cost $1,500. You then came home and over the rest of the month you went out for dinners and drinks, bought groceries, saw a couple of movies, had an unexpected car repair for $1,000, and paid $1,000 for a course (totaling $5000). That's a whopping $5,000 on your credit card. Pretend you didn't pay this off for ten years (compounding monthly), what would that look like? WARNING, this might scare you!

Most of my credit cards from banks have an APR of about 22% so let's use that for our example. Keep in mind this calculation doesn't include any additional purchases, late fees, over-limit fees, or penalty rates of interest that may apply. Gotta love that fine print stuff!

The Formula: $ Balance x (1+.22(APR in decimal format)/12(compound period, in this case 12 months))120 (to the power of the times it is compounded, in this case, 12 months x 10 years = 120)

$$\text{The Math: } \$5,000 \times (1+.22/12)^{120*}$$

*Formula provided by Business Insider

Grand Total = $44,235 (about nine times your original $5,000 in purchases!)

Compounding interest is fabulous when your money is working for you through saving and investing. However, as you can see its effects are disastrous when it works against you through interest owing. The scary part is how quick and easy it is to accumulate what feels like an impossible amount of debt to pay off.

How to Avoid Paying Credit Card Interest

Chapter Bonus:

Go to the YFF website to download my list of **simple ways to avoid paying credit card interest.**

I am super vigilant about paying my bills on time every single month, and I have never paid credit card interest (I'm also a natural planner, organizer, and Type A personality). One of my tricks that keeps me on top of my bill payments, which gets especially difficult when you have multiple cards that all have different due dates, is entering a recurring bill payment reminder for each credit card due date into my calendar for every month. I set them for a few days before the actual payment is due in case I get caught up doing something else and forget, which will leave me with a few days grace to make the payment. Even easier, some banks will allow you to set up automatic payments for the full balance of your credit card from your bank account monthly.

They're Not All Bad! Credit Card PROs

Credit cards are only a bad thing if you don't have the self-discipline to spend within your means and the organization to pay your bills on time. I love credit cards because I know how to use them and reap the benefits. I've practiced discipline in how I use them and get many great rewards. Here are some of the pros of using credit cards:

- Convenience
- Building your credit history
- Airline, hotel points, and rewards
- Amazing introductory deals such as additional points and cash-back for a certain period of time or spending amount (I've received many free flights and increased percentage in cash-back this way)
- Cash-back (getting 1-4% cash-back annually on all or some categories of your spending like groceries, gas, dining, and travel)
- Partner promotions (getting discounts at retailers and other partner companies)

- Getting on priority lists to be the first to get concert and other event tickets
- Ease of tracking and categorizing your spending
- Zero liability—allows you to dispute charges you don't recognize and withhold payments
- Consumer accident protection if your purchases are defective or accidentally broken
- Travel and other insurance benefits
- Extended warranties on purchases
- Buying shares of credit card companies (i.e. Visa, Mastercard) can be a fantastic investment – they have the power to make a lot of money!

A Reminder of Many of the Credit Cards CONs

- Ability to spend what you don't have
- You might be enticed to spend more in the moment
- Screwing up your credit score and ability to get any kind of loan/financing in the future
- Potential of credit card fraud (you must keep an eye on your charges!)
- Having too many credit cards and/or credit allowance isn't a good look in the eyes of creditors (keep your **credit utilization ratio** between 10-35 percent - *see Chapter 8 on how to rebuild your credit*)
- Not knowing how fast compounding interest owed can get out of control
- The potential stress credit card debt can cause you and your family

The benefits of using credit cards are NIL if you're not consistently paying off your balance owing in full.

Don't fall prey to marketing promotions by continuously signing up for new cards to get the introductory rewards to buy things you don't need. If you have multiple credit card balances outstanding, do some research to find a credit card company that will allow you to do a free balance transfer of the amounts owing from your other cards to simplify your payments and get a better overall interest rate. Friends don't let friends carry credit card balances!

Aside from paying nearly 0% interest on leased cars (with entrepreneurial tax advantages, of course) and mortgage interest, I vowed to never pay interest. Have I ever paid credit card interest? Nope! Once when I first got corporate credit cards for my business, I got confused with payment due dates for my personal cards and missed a payment by a few days. Simple solution: I called the bank and asked them to forgive the interest charge as I'm a loyal client, always pay on time, and explained that this was simply an organization error on my part that won't happen again. Problem solved and my interest-free life continues.

When Should I Get a Credit Card?

This is a great question with a short answer: when you're responsible enough and know how to properly use one. I got my first credit card when I was twelve years old. My parents have taught me the value of a dollar and how to maintain and build a good credit score from a very young age. When I became interested in buying my own clothes and started to go to the mall with friends after school, my mom decided to give me a monthly mall budget or credit limit of $30. With my $30, I usually got some form of cheap jewelry from Claire's or Ardene's, a tank top or t-shirt from Aritzia and a few kids ice cream cones from Purdy's Chocolates. This was quite empowering in seventh and eighth grade!

The card had my own name on it, which I thought was the coolest thing ever (although I was actually an authorized user on my mom's credit card account and it was tied to her own personal line of credit so she would know exactly what I spent my credit card allowance on every month). As an authorized user, you need to make sure you trust the person whose account you're tied to. If the primary account holder doesn't make their payments on time, it will affect your credit negatively as well (good thing Mom was vigilant about making her payments on time!)

It made me feel pretty cool amongst my friends to pull out that shiny card with my own name and signature; I loved it. The funny thing is, most kids probably thought I was a spoilt brat having a credit card and that I was lucky to have it, in spite of the fact that I told my close friends that I was only allowed to spend $30 on that card, and if I spent more there would be hell to pay at home.

At the end of the month my mom and I would go over the statement and if all the charges matched the receipts I'd saved from the mall, she would go ahead and pay the full balance on time and we'd go on to the next month. IF I spent over $30, I would either have to take the rest out of my following month's allowance or take it out of my bank account where I'd saved money doing chores to make sure we never owed interest.

I had this card for about a year and rarely ever spent more than a couple of dollars over my limit. My mom eventually canceled the card a couple of years later as I started to misplace things more often in my teenage years. She was much more worried about me losing it than spending beyond my limit.

Learning about credit cards and interest rates at such a young aged served me well. When should you get your first credit card? I've always been interested in money, finance, and getting ahead of the game so this parental experiment worked for me; but most people look at getting a credit card when they head off to college, university, or start working full-time after high school.

The credit cards pro I mentioned about introductory offers comes with a warning: read the fine print. Many credit card companies will advertise what sounds like an amazing new card offer during the first week of school at kiosks in malls, through digital marketing and cold calls, and many more avenues. They want you to be enticed by these great deals to encourage you to get a card, spend money you don't have, and then pay them interest. Credit card companies don't offer you credit and giveaway "freebies" because they're wonderful people; they are in business to make money, which could potentially come from you overspending. Your mistakes equal their profits.

We've gone over a lot about interest in this chapter, so keep this in mind when you're looking at getting your first, second, or third credit card: Is the introductory offer really worth it? In other words, would you purchase the freebie or offer anyway? Will having this additional credit burn a hole in your pocket and encourage you to spend more? Do you have the self-control to keep your eyes on the prize of a stress-free financial life?

Remember: earn to spend, not spend then earn. If you don't yet have the discipline to not overspend on credit cards (whether it's one or more), stick to cash, debit, or prepaid and secured credit cards to build your credit history so you don't spend money you don't have and incur interest charges that compound out of control. Ask your bank about **secured** and **prepaid cards** as your first step into the credit card world if you're unsure about your level of discipline!

Which Card Is Right for You?

Just prior to leaving home and moving across the country to go to university, I decided to get a credit card in order to start building my credit score and have access to credit while I was living on my own. While I was lucky enough to have my parents support me for my tuition and part of my living expenses, there was a lot I was responsible for on my own; the best way to get going was to build my own credit history as I knew this would be important for future investing, business, and day-to-day life.

There are many websites that compare credit cards to get the exact features and rewards you want. Whether you want a card without an annual fee, secured to help build your credit, one that offers price matching for large purchases, or sign up bonuses, you can search and compare cards for all of these types of features and more at a website like creditcards. com or comparecards.com. I've used these and other websites many times when considering a new card. I get sent new card offers all the time that sound amazing in the marketing materials, then I'll search one of these websites to see if there are consumer reviews, fine print I'm unaware of, or another card better suited to my needs.

Some people actually do something called **card churning** where they apply for new cards over and over again just to get the handsome sign-up bonuses; they often cancel the card afterward. I don't have the time or inclination to do this, although it goes to show that many people are recognizing and taking advantage of the offers out there.

What about Debit Cards?

Should I just use my debit card instead of using credit cards? My answer to this question would be that I would only recommend using debit cards alone if you really don't trust yourself to properly manage your credit cards. Unfortunately, debit cards don't usually provide the rewards or help build your credit history; and, unlike credit cards, if you have money stolen from your account through your debit card, you could be out of pocket for a number of weeks before your bank reconciles the fraud. With credit cards, if you call them when you notice a discrepancy in your statement, they will usually reverse the charge immediately or within a few days.

Another thing to be careful of when using your debit card is to make sure you don't use **overdraft protection** or pay any other additional fees. Be aware of your account balances often to make sure you don't get in the red. Overdraft fees can be anywhere from $20 to $50 per transaction per use, or on a monthly subscription basis. You can accumulate hundreds of dollars in fees in one day of spending if you're not aware that your account balance has dipped below $0. Keep a safety net of a couple hundred dollars in the account connected to your debit card at all times in case you overspend. I would rather have two extra happy hour sessions every month than waste money on bank fees. What would you rather have?

Summary

This is one of those "red flag" chapters with the warnings of credit card black holes. If you get into bad debt with plastic money, it not only destroys your credit, your chance to invest and be loaned cheap money (getting competitive rates on loans and mortgages) in the future, but it can send you into a quick downward spiral mentally. Debit cards and going on a cash diet or using a cash envelope spending system is always an option if you need to get yourself into the habit of spending smartly and resisting impulse purchases. However, the rewards, protections, and history that credit cards will help you build, is worth practicing disciplined spending for.

My Two Cents:

- You are not stupid! Knowing how credit cards and interest work probably wasn't taught to you in school; learn now and save yourself future pain.

- If you don't pay your entire balance on time every month, credit card companies will charge you **daily or monthly compounded interest.** That means the amount increases every day you don't pay.

- Based on a 22% **APR (annual percentage rate)** compounded monthly, a $5000 unpaid credit card balance would cost you $44,235 in ten years—approximately nine times as much!

- Always be aware of **late fees, over-limit fees, penalty rates, overdraft protection, interest,** and other fees that might apply to credit or debit cards.

- When used properly, credit cards have a lot of amazing **rewards and protections, and they build your credit history** and credit score, which is hugely important for your future.

- Try an online **website to compare different credit card rates, fees, and rewards** when looking for the right card for you.

- Can't bear the plastic money burning a hole in your wallet? Stick to debit cards or a cash diet until you build better self-control around spending.

Chapter Bonus:

Go to the YFF website to download my list of **simple ways to avoid paying credit card interest.**

Chapter 6

Sorry, but Notorious B.I.G. Had It Wrong—Mo' Money = Less problems!

"Money frees you from doing things you dislike. Since I dislike doing nearly everything, money is handy."
~ Groucho Marx

THE FAMOUS RAPPER NOTORIOUS B.I.G. had it all wrong. *Mo' Money Mo' Problems* by Biggie might have been entertaining back in the 90s (if you were born then), but if you're throwing your money around buying too many **depreciating assets** that aren't increasing your income like cars, boats, rounds of drinks for your friends every weekend, designer bags and shoes (I'm talking to you girlfriends!) . . . then you probably have less money and mo' problems. That said, if you're wise about both your spending and saving, more money definitely means less stress and more health, and allows you to live comfortably with financial independence and a lifestyle that supports your true values.

In this chapter we'll look at day-to-day banking, making compounding interest work for you, creating an emergency cushion, and other things to think about when laying the groundwork for your dream life. This starts with finding ways to save money that you may not have thought of. Remember, it all adds up.

Day-to-Day Banking

There are many different kinds of institutions where you can do your day-to-day banking transactions and where you can deposit and withdraw your money as well: big national banks, credit unions, internet banks, and trust companies. When deciding where you should keep your money, there are a few things to consider—no matter what type of institution you're looking at. Whether you're looking at opening a new account or you want to know more about the fees and policies of your current accounts, these are important things to know. People lose a lot of money to banking fees for services they don't often need or use. Do you know the answers to the following questions about your accounts?

Things to know about your bank account:

1) **Is the money in your bank accounts government insured?** Most banks and other institutions where you can open a personal or joint deposit account will have guaranteed government protection up to a certain amount if the institution fails, though you need to make sure. In the U.S. the **Federal Deposit Insurance Corporation (FDIC)** covers up to $250,000 USD per depositor, institution, and account category. The **Canadian Deposit Insurance Corporation (CDIC)** does the same in Canada for up to $100,000 CAD. If your account balance is beyond the insurance limits, look at moving some of your assets to new accounts at other institutions or into different types of account categories to make sure it's all covered. Both

corporations have easy to use coverage estimators on their websites; use them to make sure all your deposits are safe.

Note: There are similar national insurances for brokerage and investing account assets like the **Canadian Investor Protection Fund (CIPF)** and the **Securities Investor Protection Corporation (SIPC)** with similar protections for member firm eligible client assets. The key is knowing that your assets are eligible and covered.

2) **What is the interest rate?** How much money is the institution going to give you for depositing your money with them? I personally have found that internet banks, trust companies and credit unions offer the best current interest rates for my daily banking needs, and their fees are on par with the banks. Some simple comparison research online will show you the options in your area.

Chapter Bonus:

Visit the website to get a couple of great ways to **compare current bank account interest rates.**

3) **What are the fees?** What are the monthly, annual, and transaction fees for the account and do these fit your lifestyle and banking needs? Such things would include how many direct deposits, withdrawals, ATM transactions, check deposits and payments, wire and e-mail transfers are you allowed per month? Foreign exchange fees? Paper vs. online statement fees?

4) **Will you have free access to in-branch, online, app, and phone banking?** Do you require these services? Think about your lifestyle needs and how you prefer to do your banking.

5) **Minimum balance requirements?** A lot of banks require a minimum balance, particularly when they offer a higher interest rate; make sure you don't dip below this minimum amount or you'll likely be charged a penalty fee.

6) **Overdraft protection and fees?** We've all made the mistake of accidentally or knowingly spending *into the red* when we know the bank will cover our negative account balance short-term. Find out what the monthly or annual fees are for your overdraft, what the interest rate or flat fees are, if there is a pay-as-you-go option, or if there is the option to opt out of it completely if you know you're diligent enough to never go below $0.

7) **Discounts?** Are you eligible for a student, senior, military, or another discount? Save where you can.

Do Your Research! No One's Going to Give You Money If You Don't Ask!

How should you be conducting research on bank accounts and the different options and benefits available? Often people will get their first credit card from the same bank or other institution they had their first deposit account with; however, as we've seen in the last chapter it is to your advantage to shop around. The same thing goes for the different banking institutions that would be happy to hold your hard earned cash and provide you with your banking needs. They often provide added bonus incentives for opening a new account with them, using their debit cards and other services. I've seen $100 to $500 cash bonuses, travel miles, TVs and electronics, certain terms of free banking, and increased interest rates for your account. There are so many options available. A bit of research goes a long way!

Why Save? How Does Compounding Interest Work FOR You?

We know how compounding interest works against you (when you owe money—credit card debt in particular). However, when you're **earning compounding interest** in your investments and savings accounts, it works in your favor in a big way! Compounding interest is when your interest earned is added to your initial amount deposited/invested each time it's calculated. This is different from **simple interest** as simple interest is calculated one time at the end of the year/term.

While I'm going to give you an example of how much money you'd make in an average savings account with an interest rate of 1%, which sadly is good by today's standards, it is important to note that at 1% APY (**Annual Percentage Yield**: an interest rate that takes into account the effects of intra-year compounding), current interest rates aren't even matching our average **targeted inflation rate** of 2%. This means that bank account interest rates aren't keeping up with current inflation, so the cost of living is growing faster than your money is earning in interest – a losing game.

Note: APY vs. APR: Banks will quote their interest rates differently depending on what will best represent them to you, the consumer. **APR does not take into account the compounding interest** of that year, and therefore you will actually end up paying more in interest on your credit card balance, for example, than you may have initially realized or calculated. Whereas **APY does take compounding interest into account** and therefore represents the best interest you will earn by keeping money in your accounts. You can think of APR as representing the best view of interest rates on credit cards, while APY does the same for bank account interest rates.

Simple interest calculation (without compounding):
$1000 @ 1% annually = $1010.00 at the end of the year.
Compounding interest calculation (daily compounding):

$1000 @ 1% APY (annually, compounded daily)
= $1010.05 after Year 1
= $1105.17 after Year 10 = 10%

When compounded daily, 1% APY allows your deposits or investment to grow by 10% over ten years. Now imagine if you added $50, $100, or $500 to your savings account every month. If you saved an additional $100 per month over those ten years and compounded the interest daily, your ten-year total would be $13,730.93.

Chapter Bonus:

Try the **compounding interest calculator** link on the YFF website to apply the power of compounding to your own money examples.

While the figures in the example above don't seem that impressive, it's important to understand the power compounding interest has on our savings and investments over a lifetime and into retirement. These figures explode when you start calculating actual investment returns with much higher rates of return than deposits in your bank account at 1% APY. As the famous investor Robert Allen says *"How many millionaires do you know who have become wealthy by investing in savings accounts? I rest my case."*

The moral of all lessons on compounding interest: Believe in the power of time.

Start early, do it often, pay yourself first, and don't give up.

Automate your monthly savings into separate accounts for bigger goals or into your registered retirement savings plans like your 401(k) (USA) or RRSP (Canada) so you can **set it and forget it**. There are many apps that can manage your automatic savings for you or you can go to your bank and set it up directly. This takes the pressure off forcing yourself to remember to save diligently every month on your own, and you'll be motivated to continue making smart money decisions by seeing the buckets of savings you accumulate every year without even thinking about it.

Create Your Emergency Cushion

When you're trying to create a confident, secure life for yourself and your family, you need to protect yourselves from the unforeseen. The reason why many financial experts suggest creating an emergency fund or cushion is to give you the comfort in knowing you'll be okay no matter what happens—at least for a few months. Creating a cushion to give yourself the ease of knowing everything will be okay no matter what is the number one way to feel financially stress-free. Most experts suggest you should have anywhere from three to nine months of your family's basic monthly expenses saved in cash on hand for unforeseen expenses such as your car breaking down, unexpected home repairs, or in case you or your partner/spouse lose your jobs, fall ill, or otherwise.

You've already taken a solid look at your monthly needs and expenses, so flip back to your *good life work* in Chapter 4 and calculate how much your minimum monthly costs of living are. Rather than me tell you how many months of expenses you should save for, analyze your own situation and estimate how long you'd be likely to fall short of your regular household income should something happen. For my own situation, I decided three months would be an appropriate amount of time before I would likely be fully back on my feet, or able to liquidate other assets to get the cash I need to continue to support my life with less income than I had initially.

To get started on saving for your cushion, determine a monthly savings goal that's equal to 1/12 of your overall fund goal. That way, you can work at cutting back in some areas to save enough every month to have that cushion sitting in your account by this time next year. If adding this goal to your already tight monthly budget is too much, try stretching out your plan over eighteen months (1/18). Having an emergency cushion will give you the financial security and confidence you need to start working on all the other items on your Financial Nirvana timeline. Get to it!

Saving for a Goal

We just talked about how to plan and save for one particular goal, your emergency cushion. The same goes for other big-ticket items on your needs and wants lists. My first big purchase, when I really needed to work hard at saving, was for my first home's down payment. After I graduated university, I wanted to buy my first home as soon as possible. I got my first job as a financial advisor making $35,000 CAD/year (~$27,000 USD) and lived with my parents to save save save! Of course, I was extremely lucky and grateful to be able to live with my parents after school, but I was ready to move out and start real estate investing by purchasing my first place. My dad had friends who'd created an interesting solution to getting their grown children to save for their first home by starting a "rent to mortgage" fund. Rather than allowing me to live at home for free (and potentially spend all the money I was now making with a full-time job) my dad told me to pay $500/month rent and he would put it in an account specifically for my down payment savings. He didn't end up opening an actual account as I had already done all of my own research on the best rates and found that Peoples Trust provided a much higher interest rate than my bank and I opened an account myself. This is where I kept my down payment savings until I was ready to start making offers on homes. Within a year I was ready to go. I bought my first home and couldn't have been happier or more proud of myself for reaching my goal. I was also appreciative of my parents for coming up with a solid plan to encourage and support me on the journey.

Not everyone will have like-minded support from family and friends when trying to implement financial changes, which is why you need to be your own best advocate. This is when making the appropriate money decisions to meet your goals needs to become your top priority. Would you be willing to take on a roommate or two for a year in order to save for your goal? Forego the occasional big night out? Refer back to your lists of needs and wants and remind yourself of your priorities and what changes will help propel you towards your goals.

A great way to plan for a big purchase you'd like to make in the future is to find out how much you'd need to save over time; in this case, a down payment for a home. This will vary depending on your income, credit score, and other variables so you should ask a trusted mortgage broker or a mortgage specialist. Once you have a saving goal with a specific timeline to completion, after saving your emergency cushion and paying off any bad debts, you can determine the best kind of accounts, automatic savings plans, apps, and investments to use to help you achieve the goal.

Summary

There are lots of ways to save money day to day, from big-ticket spending strategies to saving on banking fees. Knowing your money situation inside and out will keep you moving toward being free from the anxieties that currently hold you back. Every little bit counts when it comes to banking fees, rewards, and interest earned in your bank accounts. It's fun and motivating to play around with some of the bonus tools mentioned in this chapter to see how your money can grow when you really start investing in yourself and your future. Now that we've covered the foundations, the next step is to show you how to make your money work for you through investing. My favorite topic!

My Two Cents:

- Things to know about your bank account: Is it government insured? What's the interest rate? Fees? Do they have in-branch, online, app, and phone banking? Minimum balance requirements? Overdraft protection and fees? Discounts?

- **Compounding interest** is when your interest earned is added to your initial amount deposited/invested each time it's calculated. Interest on interest!

- **Set it and forget it. Automate your savings and investing contributions every month** out of your income before you start to spend. This is called **paying yourself first!**

- **The moral of all lessons on compounding interest:** Believe in the power of time.

- **Simple interest** is calculated one time at the end of the year/term.

- **APR vs. AYR:** Be aware that banks quote rates on loans, credit cards, and interest to their advantage; know that **APR does not take compounding interest into account,** whereas **APY does compound daily/monthly.**

- Create an **emergency cash cushion** of at least three months of your household expenses, should you/your partner lose your jobs or fall ill, to give yourself and your family security.

- Setting goals and timelines for savings—like your Financial Nirvana timeline—will help you stay motivated to reach your goals.

Chapter Bonuses:

1) Go to the YFF website for my two favorite websites to **compare current bank account interest rates.**

2) Try the **compounding interest calculator** link on the website to apply the power of compounding to your own money examples.

Chapter 7

Investing Basics: Now that You Have Some Dough, Let's Make It Grow!

"What's worth doing is worth doing for money."
~ Gordon Gekko (Michael Douglas) *Wall Street*

NOW THAT YOU KNOW the basics of how to spend, save, and create an emergency cushion, you're at a place where you can start to get excited about investing your hard earned cash and watching it grow. People tend to get very overwhelmed at this stage in the road to financial wellness. I don't blame you. There are so many different products, opinions, and strategies out there about portfolio management, diversification, allocations, etc. This chapter will cover the basics: myths about finance and investing, types of income and which is the most valuable, how to build your empire through investing, and some basics about various types of investment products and their different levels of risk and reward. Let's talk about the things that wealthy people do to go from being comfortable to being "rich".

Three Myths about Investing

The most common hurdle I come across with those new to investing is *fear*. People think that investing is too complex, or they don't have enough money to get started, or that investing is too risky. Let's take a look at these three myths and see why they're wrong so they don't continue to hold you back from your dream lifestyle.

Financial Myth #1: It's too complicated! I don't know enough to invest! I hear this all too often, including from highly educated professionals all over the world. As I've said, not everyone had a natural interest in reading investment books when they were children or teenagers (lucky me!); however, a little bit of knowledge goes a long way. If you're three-quarters of the way through this book, you're already much further ahead than the majority of society. You have the drive and commitment to read this so, believe me, you can quite easily learn enough about investing to create substantial earnings for your future. It often seems very complicated at first because there are so many different types of investment product asset classes, which we'll go over later in this chapter; however, if you know the basic principles behind **why** you're investing, **what** your goals are, and what your **level of risk** tolerance is, it all falls into place from there. Invest in yourself, your knowledge, and the right skills to get where you want to be financially—you're already halfway there.

Financial Myth #2: I don't have enough money to start investing! Although we haven't gone over the different elements of debt yet, if you have managed to stay debt free, or paid off the high-interest bad debts from your past, like payday loans and credit cards, and saved an emergency cushion, you're ready to start investing. Often people don't realize there are many different ways to actually purchase financial products and/or invest your money in other ways. There are many ways to get started: buying and selling investments on your own through an online discount brokerage, working with a financial advisor, buying real estate assets, starting a new business, or private investment vehicles. They all have different entry points in terms of minimum investment required, fees, service, risk, and available research.

Depending on how you want to **diversify** your investments, you may need more money to have a good asset mix so you can allocate your investment dollars into different **asset classes** (different types of investments, see infographic below). This ensures that your money isn't too heavily concentrated in one area or another, but we'll cover that later. To get started in investing, I recommend first having your bad debts paid off, a minimum three-month emergency cash cushion saved, and then setting $1000 aside to invest. That's it, $1000!

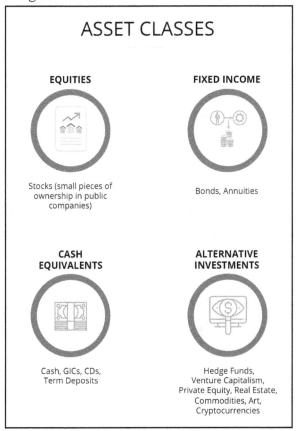

ASSET CLASSES

EQUITIES

Stocks (small pieces of ownership in public companies)

FIXED INCOME

Bonds, Annuities

CASH EQUIVALENTS

Cash, GICs, CDs, Term Deposits

ALTERNATIVE INVESTMENTS

Hedge Funds, Venture Capitalism, Private Equity, Real Estate, Commodities, Art, Cryptocurrencies

Financial Myth #3: Investing is too risky! This one makes me laugh! If you think investing is risky, think of the kind of risk you're taking on by not investing for your future. I'm not talking solely about retirement investments; I'm referring to investing to generate income for the next five to ten years. I personally have the majority of my portfolio in equities (individual stocks and funds) and real estate due to my age, personality, and level of risk tolerance. I don't recommend investing in individual companies to people who don't have a keen interest and knowledge of the stock market, and who don't have the time to do the proper research. However, there is an investing style that fits everyone no matter how **risk averse** you are. The fact of the matter is that at current interest rates, your money sitting in your bank account is likely earning 1% interest or less, which means the value of your money isn't even keeping up with targeted inflation of 2 to 3%. That said, you're actually losing purchasing power by letting your cash sit in your bank account. You're not doing your family any favors by putting them at risk of needing to take care of you financially in retirement. Not to mention losing out on the opportunity to realize incredible returns throughout the rest of your life, to be able to actually have fun with your money (!) if you start taking on a small amount of risk to invest now.

When it comes to these three myths, I hope they've been debunked and given you some confidence that YOU CAN start investing now, and it will be worth it.

Three Types of Income: Earned, Portfolio, and Passive; Why Passive Is the Best

These are the three broad types of income we generate throughout our lives. Let's take a look at each (passive income is the preferred type of income wealthy people strive to build throughout their lives). Income includes all wages, salaries, interest earned, commissions, royalties, dividends, profits, rental income, and any other way you receive money.

Income can be fixed or variable. An example of **fixed income** would be your annual salary at your day job where you make a fixed amount. **Variable income** is often business income or side hustle income where depending on different business factors your income will vary from year to year. The best way to diversify your income and have multiple sources of money coming in is to create different types of income through your job, side hustles, and investing.

1) **Earned Income—Sometimes Called Active**: Whether you are generating income through your job or a business, this is called *earned income*. Any money you receive as a result of your time put into working for yourself or someone else is earned. The downside to earned income is, although it is the most common type of income, it's often the most highly taxed and your income is limited to the amount of time and effort you commit. Earned income is usually the starter money that allows people to save in order to start their own businesses or invest and make more money later on. Here are some examples of earned income:

   • Employee pay including: wages, salaries, tips, etc.

   • Owning your own small business (this tax structure would be different than job income)

   • Consulting and self-employed side hustles

   • Disability, union strike pay, and other benefits income

2) **Portfolio Income—Sometimes Called Capital Gains**: Most people use their earned income to build a portfolio of other investments that will bring them

additional income. Portfolio income is any investment that you buy for one price and sell for more,
making a profit. In many cases, the longer you hold
an investment in your portfolio the better your tax
rate will be on the gain when you sell the investment/
asset. Taxation on different types of portfolio income
can vary, sometimes it's much better than earned
income but sometimes it can be just as high. You may
also require a higher level of initial investment, for
example in real estate, as well as knowledge or expertise in a certain field. Some examples of investments
that can be bought and sold to generate portfolio
income include:

- Paper assets such as stocks, bonds, mutual funds,
  ETFs (Exchange-Traded Funds), CDs (Certificate of Deposit – USA), GIC (Guaranteed
  Investment Certificate – CAD), index funds,
  T-bills (Treasury Bills), futures and derivatives
  (now we're getting complicated!), currencies, and
  commodities

- Real estate, buying and selling

- Other physical assets like cars, antiques, jewelry,
  art

3) **Passive Income**: This is the mecca of all wealth
   building! Passive income is great, as it's typically gen-
   erated from something you acquired as an asset or
   a business you created over a certain period of time
   that will continue to generate income for a lifetime
   (or a long time). This income is passive because once
   you've put the initial work in, the business or asset
   itself does the rest of the work and requires only minimal to no effort to earn more money. This is different
   than *earned* business income, as earned income would
   mean you are continuing to put more personal work

hours into the business to generate that income. Passive income also is usually consistent, recurring, and predictable. Generations of wealth and prosperity are built on passive income. The IRS defines passive income as *"rental activity or trade or business activities in which you do not materially participate."* Here are some examples:

- Real estate rental income
- Recurring commissions
- Inactive royalties
- Affiliate marketing
- Dividend-paying stocks

What and Where Should I Start?

I hope you're getting more comfortable with the prospect of starting to invest. If you've made it this far and you're actually considering starting to invest, that's great. You are way ahead of most people and now have the ability to start building wealth to support your dream lifestyle and your family's future.

So you have $1000 cash idly sitting in your low interest bearing account. What next? The first thing to consider when investing is **what** and **where** you're going to invest your money. Let's start with the **what**. Most beginner investors usually start by investing in mutual funds, bonds, ETFs, and maybe stocks (shares in individual companies). I wouldn't recommend this last option unless you have enough time to do the proper research.

The place I recommend newbies start investing is in index funds and ETFs. A **mutual fund** is a type of investment vehicle that invests in a basket of different assets such as bonds and stocks. **Index funds** are a type of mutual fund, a basket of assets that are designed to mirror/track the performance of an overall index of stocks or a market like the Standard and Poor's 500 (S&P 500) or the Toronto Stock Exchange (TSX). The reason I favor index funds when you're starting out is because they historically offer better returns over time for a much lower cost because they are passively managed and charge lower management fees, whereas traditional mutual funds are actively managed and have higher fees. Over the long-term, annual returns of index funds are on average ~7 to 10%, or close to the overall performance of the index or market itself. Traditional index funds can be bought through a representative at your bank or brokerage just like any other kind of mutual fund.

Index investing through **Exchange-Traded Funds (ETFs)** that track an index like the S&P 500 or TSX offers similar advantages as traditional index funds and are more convenient for investors because you can buy them on your own at home, online through your discount brokerage account (i.e. "exchange-traded"). Although whether you choose traditional index mutual funds or index ETFs, be prepared to see your returns go up and down over the years as the markets experience change. Your overall long-term returns will still be much higher than the average returns of other types of actively managed mutual funds which are closer to ~3% (close to the current rate of inflation).

One of the biggest benefits of passive investing through index funds and ETFs are their low fees or **expense ratios** called the **Management Expense Ratio (MER)** near 0%, as compared to actively managed mutual funds at approximately 2%. Index funds and ETFs are passively managed meaning there isn't a fund manager or team of managers actively managing the fund on a daily basis; actively managed mutual or other funds incur higher fees for investors.

There has been a passive management evolution over the past ten years with investors continuing to move their funds from actively managed mutual funds to passive index funds and ETFs. According to Moody's Investors Services, passive investments now account for over 28% of all **assets under management (AUM)** in the USA, and $6 trillion dollars in assets globally. The outflows from active funds and inflows to passive funds have picked up steam much faster in the USA than Canada, however, the theme is expected to continue as actively managed funds continue to underperform major indexes like the S&P 500 and the TSX (Toronto Stock Exchange). That said, there are many highly qualified fund managers whom I've worked with that are able to outperform the market, depending on their strategy, state of current economics, and the type of fund or investment portfolio they are managing. Often this is seen in **alternative investments** like **hedge funds**, **private equity**, and **venture capitalism**. Traditionally, these types of investments have been much more complex and only available to experienced investors, however, some fund companies are developing new investment products geared toward younger investors. This is definitely a space to watch!

4 Reasons to Invest in Index Funds and ETFs

1) **Good Returns** (7-10%+)

2) **Low Fees** (less than 1%)

3) **Broad Market Exposure** – the opportunity to have broad investment exposure to different markets like the USA, Canadian, European, emerging markets and global equities or bonds, and sectors like real estate, commodities, foreign currency, energy, healthcare, etc.

4) **Cheap Diversification** – with so many different types of ETFs available it is an easy way to create your own well-diversified portfolio on the cheap!

With any investment, particularly if you are interested in taking the time to invest in individual stocks, I recommend **five investing principles to live by:**

1) **Buy and hold**; Invest for the long-term. For the average investor, speculating in short-term investments (anything less than one year) is a really bad idea and is not actual investing—it's just that, speculation. Yes, I have made this mistake before after being talked into "easy wins" by friends and stockbrokers—they all lost 50% or more. Buy companies that won't be obsolete when you retire.

2) **Buy companies with experienced management teams.**

3) **Minimize fees**; one of the main reasons why I like index funds and ETF's.

4) **Minimize taxes**; such as capital gains, dividends, and inheritance. I use a tax-free trading account for all my individual stock purchases.

5) **Invest with your brain, not your emotions**; don't let your fear and emotions control your investing decisions, particularly when it comes to selling.

Again, if you don't know enough about how to invest in individual stocks which takes a lot of research and time, buying ETFs on your own, or index funds through your bank or brokerage are your best ways to get started. When you add in the power of your returns compounding over many years, index investments will give you a solid start at building a quality investment portfolio.

Much of my learning about investing and the stock market early on was through watching *Mad Money* on CNBC every day and excitedly taking notes as the unconventional and brilliant teacher Jim Cramer rattled on about various investing topics and stock picks. One of his most basic investing rules is that your first $10,000 should be invested in index funds. Many fund managers and financial advisors don't like to suggest index funds or ETFs to their clients as they don't generate the same amount of fees and commissions for the bank and its managers as actively managed mutual funds do. Don't let this fool you! Ask the right questions, do the math yourself, and then decide if you'd rather invest in actively or passively managed funds.

In one of his recent 2017 episodes addressing generational investing, Jim said that from 1928 through 2014, the S&P 500 index produced an average annual return of 10%, including dividends. That might not sound that fantastic, but thanks to the magic of compounding, a 10% annual return will double your money in about seven years. Furthermore, if you invested $1,000 in an ETF or index fund tracking the S&P 500 today, 40 years from now that investment could be worth over $45,000 – not too shabby! (Remember to check out the compound interest calculator on the YFF website to play around with your own potential investment returns).

Rise of the Robots

Want to take the work out of investing all together? Don't think you have enough assets? Feel intimidated by advisors? Or don't want to pay for a fully comprehensive investment plan from a professional (the average cost of this is approximately $1900 USD)? Then an online **robo-advisor** might be a good option for you. It would be really cool if there were rooms full of robots running around managing your money, however, they're not actually robots, but software platforms full of algorithms developed by some of the best minds in finance that use automation to manage your investments. Robo-advisors are a convenient, low-cost way of investing in a diversified portfolio of **ETFs (exchange-traded funds)** without you yourself having to think of what markets or industries you should invest in to have a diversified portfolio. You may have heard of some of the most popular robos like Betterment and Wealthfront (USA) and Wealthsimple or Questrade Portfolio IQ (Canada).

One problem, however, is that robo-advisors don't replace the important component of getting personal, professional one on one human advice from a qualified advisor to help you adjust for big life and economic changes like getting married, having children, purchasing real estate, or going through a recession. Other considerations for your overall financial planning and ultimately retirement, would be if you have a pension, social security, inheritance, future or current dependents, tax planning, and many others which robos won't be able to help you with.

I really enjoy investing, so I prefer a DIY approach to buying ETFs, stocks and other investments on my own or with the help of advice directly from a financial advisor. Although I do think that even just going through the initial exercise of completing one of the robos online questionnaires can be helpful in determining what your initial investment allocations should be when you're first starting to invest.

How Much Risk Can You Handle?

An important point to remember—before determining where to put your money—is your level of **risk tolerance**. How **risk averse** (reluctant to take on risk) are you? How old are you? Are you close to retirement? What are your standing financial commitments? Do you have a large expenditure coming up for which you'll need access to the cash you're considering investing? What are your future lifestyle goals?

The answers to these questions will guide you to an asset class or type of investment that's best suited to your needs and, more importantly, what level of return your investments require for you to be able to reach your goals. If you're working with a financial advisor or broker, they will (or should) review this with you when making investment decisions.

For example, I'll be 30 when this book is published, single, no kids, have no bad debts, own real estate and other investments, and I'm financially literate; therefore, I consider myself highly risk tolerant. If your situation is different, and it is for every single one of us, your investment decisions will and should be different than mine. Keep in mind that rates of return are typically a function of risk (i.e. bigger risks = bigger rewards). You will be best served by taking on riskier investments like **equities** (shares of private and public companies) when you're younger and tapering those off into more secure, stable investments like **bonds** (a debt instrument where the issuer promises to pay you back your principal plus interest at a certain date) as you age closer to retirement. I could go on about this topic forever. It's extremely important to assess your own personal situation before making any investment decisions.

Let's Talk about Fees Baby!

One of the most important things to decide is how much you're willing to pay in fees to buy, sell, and manage your investments. Depending on what you want to invest in, you might be able to buy and sell investment products on your own very inexpensively through an online discount brokerage. This is called **self-directed investing**. This is what I personally use to buy and sell individual stocks and ETFs (exchange-traded funds) because it's cheap, easy to use, and it's simple to open an account. Some of the best, and names you may have heard of include Questrade, Qtrade, and BMO InvestorLine (Canada); and Charles Schwab, Scottrade, E*Trade, Fidelity, Ally Invest, Stockpile, and Robinhood (USA). Do your research online to see which companies offer the types of accounts, research and advisory services, and fees that best suit your needs.

Commissions (transaction fees) to buy and sell investments online at discount brokerages range from $0 to $10+. They also offer a range of minimum account balances required to open an account, usually about $0 to $5000. To give you an example of the savings to be realized through discount brokers, I opened my first brokerage account at my bank (where trades to buy or sell stocks, ETFs and any other investment available was over $40/trade). I did this because it was the easiest and first option I had when I was starting out, as it was suggested to me by my banker and set up for me in my branch in ten minutes. Shortly thereafter, I did some research about online discount brokerages and compared their trading fees, account minimums, low activity fees, and types of accounts available on a few comparison sites, found the best one for me, and opened an account for free where I paid a flat fee of $4.95/trade. This meant big savings for a small investor like me.

However, it's important to know that online discount brokerages have limited product offerings that can be bought and they won't provide you with the full-service advisory help you would get (and might need) from a trusted fiduciary (USA), financial advisor, or broker.

A **fiduciary** is an American term for a financial advisor who is legally obligated to make investment decisions that are in their clients' best interest (rather than potentially being able to sell you investment products because they generate a higher commission or fee). This is an important concept to understand because if you are an in the USA you should be 100% sure that your advisor is indeed required to act as a fiduciary at ALL times when they are giving you investment advice. Unsure? Ask them.

If you're learning about new investment products, diversification, planning your overall portfolio or a major life change, it's best to look at full-service companies in your area or be committed to doing a lot of the learning on your own.

Start by asking questions about investment options and fees of the folks at your local bank that you already have a relationship with, and continue your research from there.

Another thing I did when I was starting to learn about investing in my teens was going to free lunch and learn workshops that were held at my bank's local branch. I went to all of them covering various investing topics. I was the youngest person there, no doubt about it, taking the most notes (as usual) and it taught me a lot—the basics at least. Ask your bank next time you're in if there are any free workshops or seminars you could attend to get some in-person learning and ask questions. Don't be embarrassed to be a keener!

Your human resources team at work should also be a go-to place for potential financial literacy education. Aside from your company sponsored 401(k) or RRSP plan, many organizations are (or should be) implementing employee financial wellness benefits like workshops and other resources in the workplace to increase employee productivity, decrease turnover, and create a culture where employees feel valued and cared for. This is an area of my own business that I'm extremely passionate about and I hope will continue to grow as employers see the value in an educated, productive, decreased stress workforce.

I love hearing people's stories of success, so feel free to contact me anytime through **www.youngfunfree.com** if you have a success story to share about your own investing experiences.

Chapter Bonus:

For more information on the different types of investment classes and products available, check out the website for a list of **Investing Terms and Products to Know**.

Summary

Don't let media and marketing scare you away from investing. Just as your money should bring you confidence and security, investing your money does the same; it's empowering to know that investing isn't too complicated for you to start putting your money to work, you do have enough funds to get started, and that the real risk in investing is not doing it at all.

You might feel like you've been hit with a lot of information in this chapter, which is true. Don't worry about feeling overwhelmed; it packs a big punch and it's totally normal if you're new to investing. Use this as your playbook to building a wealthy future. Refer back to this chapter to re-familiarize yourself with the three different types of income (earned, portfolio, and passive), the four main asset classes (equities, cash, fixed income, and alternatives) and the five principles of investing over time as you start to consider your different options.

Not ready to invest yet? If you have bad debts like credit cards, payday loans, high-interest rate student or car loans, jump over to Chapter 8 where we'll look at getting back to ground zero before you start investing.

My Two Cents:

- **Busting the 3 Myths about Investing**:
  1. Investing isn't too complicated
  2. Investing isn't too risky
  3. You do have enough money to start investing
- 3 Types of Income:
  1. Earned
  2. Portfolio
  3. Passive—passive is often the least taxed and effort required

- **Index funds** are a type of passive mutual fund that are designed to mirror the performance of an overall index of stocks or a market.

- **Exchange-traded funds (ETF)** are low-cost passive investment funds you can buy yourself online.

- **3 Reasons to Invest in Index Funds and ETFs:**
  1. **Good Returns** (7-10%)
  2. **Low Fees** (less than 1%)
  3. **Broad Market Exposure**

- **4 Major Asset Classes**
  1. Equities
  2. Cash
  3. Fixed income
  4. Alternatives

- **5 Investing Principles to Live By**
  1. Buy and hold
  2. Buy companies with experienced management teams
  3. Minimize fees
  4. Minimize taxes
  5. Invest with your brain, not your emotions

- **Risk Tolerance**—know yours by your age, income, personality, and values

- **Get a Fiduciary**— In the USA, know that your financial advisor is legally obligated to act in your best interest at all times. In Canada, find a **CFP (Certified Financial Planner)** or a qualified financial advisor you have a trusted referral for.

Chapter Bonus:

For more information on the types of investment classes and products available, go to the YFF website for a list of **Investing Terms and Products to Know.**

Chapter 8

Getting to Ground Zero: Paying off Your Debt and Restoring Your Credit

"A bank is a place that will lend you money if you can prove that you don't need it."
~ Bob Hope

WE'VE NOW LEARNED ABOUT many different topics within the financial wellness arena. Step 4 on the Path to Financial Nirvana is taking action. Getting back to zero and being bad debt-free or *in the black* is the biggest part of that step. We've seen the good, the bad, and now the ugly—debt. Debt, whether it's good or bad debt, adds a lot of weight on anyone's shoulders. Debt can be detrimental to your health so it's important to really let this chapter soak in if you are starting from a place of debt. The stress, sleepless nights, and worry that bad debts cause are a danger to your physical and mental health, but most importantly, it is 100% avoidable. In many cases, short-term debt is unavoidable like student loans if you don't have family financial support in your pursuit of higher education. Or imagine a cash-only world where you had to book travel, pay for transportation, and your living expenses all by cash—near impossible! The convenience of credit cards makes life a whole lot easier IF you are fully paying off your balances owing when they're due every month. In this chapter I'll show you how to get back in the black.

The Big D—DEBT

Most people I know or have worked with who have some kind of debt feel overwhelmed by the stress of it because they don't have a sound plan on how to get out of debt. They don't see the light at the end of the tunnel. My greatest hope, if you're in this situation, is that this chapter will bring you not only light and hope for a wonderful future, but the tools and insights to make a plan to put a dent in your debt, and to live a life you truly deserve.

Different Types of Debt—the Good, the Bad, and the Ugly

Before I jump into discussing this subject, here is an excellent, simplified infographic that explains Good vs. Bad debt:

Good debt? Yes! There is such a thing! **Good debt** is typically considered a loan taken out to acquire an asset that will increase in value over time **(appreciates)** or a loan that provides the funds for an investment in your future. Good debt loans are also often given at a much lower interest rate than most bad debts. Some examples of good debts are:

- Mortgages (real estate investing)
- Home Equity Loan/Line of Credit (LOC) (adding value to your real estate through upgrades and renovations)
- Minimal Student Loans (higher education)
- Business Loans (small business opportunities)
- RRSP/401(k) Loans (for other forms of investing) **Note:** This is a controversial subject depending on many factors

GOOD DEBT VS. BAD DEBT
– What's Yours?

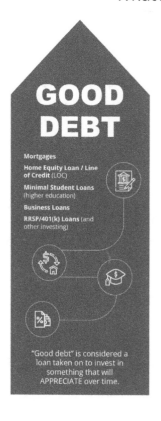

GOOD DEBT

Mortgages

Home Equity Loan / Line of Credit (LOC)

Minimal Student Loans (higher education)

Business Loans

RRSP/401(k) Loans (and other investing)

"Good debt" is considered a loan taken on to invest in something that will APPRECIATE over time.

"Bad debt" is a debt for anything that decreases in value/ DEPRECIATES or doesn't increase your net worth or income.

Payday Loans

Credit Card Debt

Medical Bills

Car Loans

Gambling Debts

Consumer Loans

BAD DEBT

Even though the above are all excellent reasons to have debt, none of these things are guaranteed positive investments and worth the interest payments and potential hit to your credit score if things go south and you end up missing payments. A lot of people don't end up needing or using their education, real estate and financial markets change all the time, and 50 percent of small businesses fail within their first five years.

So why take the leap? As mentioned in our investing chapter, risk is most often correlated with reward so if you do take risks in these areas and acquire some shorter-term, low-interest-rate debt to try it (with a sound plan), then it could end up being a big reward. Go for your dreams and make them happen! Life isn't worth living without taking some risk. Especially when the reward could be so much bigger than the alternative of doing nothing and getting nothing.

As for the big, bad, and ugly, **bad debt** is anything that decreases in value **(depreciates)** the minute you buy it, and/or doesn't increase your net worth or income. Worst of all, bad debt is usually expensive and can be detrimental to your future in terms of your credit score and ability to get approved for loans of any kind. Examples:

- Payday loans
- Credit card debt
- Medical bills
- Car loans
- Gambling debts
- Consumer loans (personal consumer loans are most often providing for unnecessary clothes, vacations, housing and transportation expenses, consumables, and other services—living beyond your means!)

Carrying credit card balances is the devil of debts and it's all in the details. The compounding interest, fees, and other hidden charges you weren't aware of can spiral out of control so quickly it makes it almost impossible to keep up (or so you thought). Payday loans, and gambling debts are terrible as well, although less common. If you have some bad debt on the books and are sick of dealing with debt collectors, looming bankruptcy, wage garnishment, and all the other associated stresses, let's look at two great ways to start paying down your debt and getting your dream life back on track.

Where Do I Start? The Snowball vs. Avalanche Methods

According to NerdWallet's 2016 annual survey of American household debt, the average credit card, auto loan, and student loan debts owed was a combined $97,048 USD! This is excluding mortgages and all other types of loans! An increase of 11 percent over the past decade. The ball and chain that debt creates is an unnecessary life stressor. Whether you are looking to pay down good or bad debts (always start with the bad), there are two common debt reduction strategies that are widely recommended:

1. **The Snowball Method**: The debt-snowball method suggests that paying off smaller debts first will give you the confidence and motivation to keep moving forward to eventually pay down your larger debts, regardless of their interest rates. Rather than paying off your debts by simply looking at which one has the highest interest rate, you would make a list of all your debts and balances owing in ascending order, pay off the smallest balance first, then the second smallest, and so on. While doing this, you would also make the minimum payments on the other debts owing. The theory behind this is that the psychological momen-

tum your snowball builds as you tackle these smaller debts will eventually help you pay down your larger debts. Although this goes against my mathematical mind, it has worked for many people including incredible success stories of people I know, and many financial experts advocate this method.

2. **The Avalanche Method:** Sometimes referred to as the *debt stacking method*, the   Avalanche method focuses on paying off your highest interest rate debts first, like credit cards and payday loans, regardless of the size of the balance owing. This method makes the most mathematical sense in terms of how much money you're actually spending on interest payments, and will cost you less to get debt free. If you have the financial discipline to know you will stick to your plan, and the commitment to paying off your debts, this method will work best for you.

It's difficult to choose one or the other as an expert because both methods will work well for different personality types. Which one will work best for you? Why not try a mix of both? Pay off one or two of your smaller balances owing first (snowball method) to get yourself motivated, then switch over to the avalanche method and tackle your highest interest rate debts. Once you've paid off your bad debts you can start putting that money toward saving and investment goals for the things you really want. Even more reason to attack that debt aggressively!

Something to consider: If you're looking to pay down debts, enlist the **accountability partner** you confided in while creating your Financial Nirvana timeline to help keep you on track. Teach them about how you plan to pay down your debts and the strategies you will implement to make it happen. They might even be able to give you some suggestions as to how you can make other small changes to pay it down even faster!

Should I Be Saving While Paying off My Debts?

The answer to this question depends on your situation. If you already have an emergency cushion saved, then you should focus your efforts on paying down your high-interest-rate debts and making the minimum payment on your other debts in order to not hurt your credit score any further. In Chapter 6 on savings, I talked about my own three-month cushion. Again, depending on your family situation, you might not feel comfortable until you have six or nine months of monthly expenses saved. After you reach this point, you can crush your debts like they deserve! Always make sure to protect yourself and your family first, followed by restoring your credit and investing after.

Chapter Bonus:

Which debt reduction method best suits you? Go to the YFF website to download your own **Snowball and Avalanche Plan** to help you decide.

FICO What? Why Should I Care? What It Affects? Who Sees It?

So if you've been carrying some debt around or missed some payments here and there, that may have already screwed up your credit score; let's talk about why it matters, and how to redeem yourself in the eyes of creditors. This is super important if you'll ever need to borrow money for a good reason again or have your credit checked. Here is a list of some reasons why your credit gets checked and why it's so important to keep your credit score IN check!

What's at risk when you have a bad credit score?

- Education loans

- Buying a home

- Starting a business

- Opening a new phone, utilities, or credit card account

- Applying for a new apartment lease

- Job applications

- Purchasing or leasing a car

- Potentially higher insurance premiums

- Higher interest rates and fees on all types of loans

- Strain on your personal relationships! Increased stress!

The **FICO Score** is the credit score used to assess your personal level of credit risk. It is used to determine whether or not the lender or creditor believes you will be able to pay your debts if they were to issue you more credit. The FICO Score was introduced by the Fair, Isaac Corporation in 1989 as a way to standardize consumer credit scores across North America's **three national credit reporting companies (CRCs) Equifax, TransUnion,** and **Experian** (USA only). Credit scales range depending on the country you're in and which scoring model or reporting company is being used, but generally if you have a credit score of 650 or higher (up to 850, 900, or even over 1000 with some models) you would be considered to have very good credit history. If your credit score is lower than 650, you might be subject to higher interest rates or you won't be offered the loan amount you need or want if the lender isn't willing to take on the risk.

The more recently introduced **VantageScore,** created by Equifax, TransUnion, and Experian, uses trended data to track the trajectory of your debt on a month-to-month basis. With the VantageScore system, this means that a person who is gradually paying down their debts would be rated higher than someone who is only paying the minimum payments while slowly gaining more debt. While VantageScore continues to gain acceptance by the majority of major financial institutions, 90 percent loan decisions are still based on FICO scores (according to NerdWallet).

Take a look at the infographic below to see the importance of the different components of your credit score.

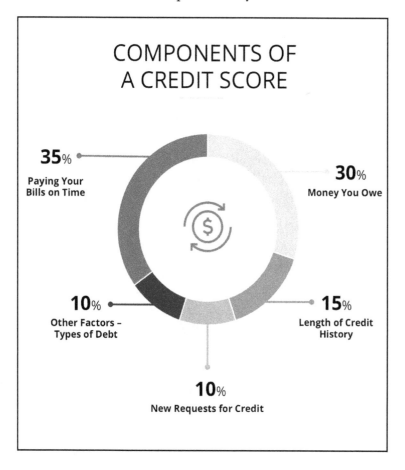

From seeing the information above, hopefully, you can better understand how having bad credit will affect your life and financial goals—even once you've overcome your debts. Part of getting back to ground zero in your financial life is **rebuilding your credit score** to be able to access the same rates and opportunities as a person with an excellent score. To get there, there are many things you can do.

Tips and Tricks to Rebuilding Your Credit Score

- **Request a copy of and monitor your credit report** from Equifax, TransUnion, or Experian (USA only). There is typically a small single-request fee or a subscription service if you'd like to monitor changes in your score. When you receive your report, read the *risk factor statements* that will tell you exactly what issues you need to fix in order to improve your credit score. There are also many online resources where you can get your FICO score or VantageScore without the full report for free like Credit Karma (.com/.ca).

- **Start paying your bills on time!** Bill payment history accounts for 35 percent of your FICO Score; set recurring reminders for yourself for your credit card bills and other payments in your phone's calendar. Better yet, set up pre-authorized payments for as many monthly bills as you can to make sure you're paying on time. There are also lots of apps you can download to track your payments as well.

- **How much do you currently owe?** Keep your owed balances low. Your amounts currently owed account for 30 percent of your credit score.

- **Don't close cards you don't use.** Cut up the cards and leave the accounts open. Closing the account itself can cause a dent in your credit history.

- New to credit? **Don't take every credit card offered to you.** Opening too many credit accounts too quickly can also damage your score rather than diversifying your credit availability. If you have bad or no credit, try starting off with a **secured card,** which requires a cash deposit before you can spend. Your credit limit then becomes the amount you deposit and allows you to make purchases while building your credit history. You can also become an **authorized user** on someone else's account (see Chapter 5 for my personal example).

- **Watch your Credit Utilization Ratio** (the ratio of your total credit used to your total credit limit). Using 10-35 percent of your monthly available credit is the ideal range to rebuild credit. For example, if you have 2 credit cards each with credit limits of $5,000 and you've spent $2,000 on one card and $1,000 on the other, your Utilization Ratio is $3,000/$10,000 = 30 percent.

How Long Will It Take?

This is a tough question as it's situation specific and depends on the severity of your former financial situation (bankruptcy, collections, repossession, foreclosure, legal judgments). For negative credit events and major issues, there is a maximum number of years they remain on your credit report, usually six to ten years. If your former setbacks weren't as severe, and you stay committed to using the strategies previously mentioned, you can quite easily get your credit back in good standing within six months to a year.

Beware of Credit Quick Fixes: There are many sources on the internet and even over the phone that will tout "credit fixing" services. These services are usually offered at hundreds of dollars and there is no way they can do anything to fix blemishes on your credit report, other than remove errors from the report which you can easily do yourself free of charge. They're not all bad, but most likely not worth your time or money.

A nonprofit agency I've heard good reviews of for American readers is Clearpoint. They offer online, phone, and in-person credit, budgeting, bankruptcy and housing counseling for reasonable fees.

Summary

This chapter is definitely the heaviest portion of the take-action-steps-toward-your-dream-life work. There is really nothing fun or exciting about debt or credit scores (sorry to everyone who works in these fields). That's just my opinion. It is, however, the first area of your financial life to get in order if needed.

There are other ways to make paying down your debts easier, like debt refinancing and consolidating. **Consolidation** is when you combine your debts or loans into one single loan making it easier to manage your payments. However, you might not save any money. When you **refinance,** you're actually rolling all your loans or debts into a completely new loan—at a lower interest rate to reduce the amount of interest you'll be paying overall.

I recommend taking a look at SoFi.com or Common-Bond.co for student loan refinancing and consolidation options to be able to pay off your debt faster and cheaper. You should also ask your bank or credit card providers directly about options they can offer you in terms of consolidating or refinancing your debts at a lower rate. No company is going to call you and ask you if you want to pay them less money. You must ask for it.

My goal for this book is to get you thinking about where

you want to be, so you can then create a plan that reflects your true values and how you will make it happen. Dream about what you want your life to look like and decide if the work is worth it. I assure you it is, but that's your own personal decision to make.

Are you more of a snowball or avalanche thinker? Do you know if your credit is in good standing? In order to take control of your financial life and have the security you deserve, it's important to think about these things and how they affect you and your family. This leads into the next chapter on how to protect yourself and your family in case of an unforeseen crisis.

My Two Cents:

- The stress, sleepless nights, and worry caused by bad debt are a danger to your physical health and productivity, but, most importantly, it is 100 percent avoidable.

- **Good debt** is a loan taken out to acquire an asset that will increase in value or your income over time **(appreciates).**

- **Bad debt** is anything that decreases in value **(depreciates)** the minute you buy it, and/or doesn't increase your net worth or income.

- Credit card debt is the devil of all debts because of compounding interest, fees, and other hidden charges.

- The **Snowball Method** suggests that knocking off smaller debts first will give you the confidence and motivation to keep moving forward to getting rid of larger debts.

- The **Avalanche Method** focuses on paying off your highest interest rate debts first, like credit cards and payday loans, regardless of the size of the balance owing.

- **FICO Score** is the credit score used by most lenders to assess your personal level of credit risk.

- **Rebuilding your credit score** is important to be able to access the same rates and life opportunities as a person with an excellent score.

- By implementing the many tools and strategies in this chapter, you can likely restore your credit to good standing within a year!

Chapter Bonus:

Which debt reduction method best suits you? Go to the YFF website to download your own **Snowball and Avalanche Plan** to help you decide.

"You don't learn to walk by following rules.
You learn by doing and falling over."
~ Sir Richard Branson

Chapter 9

Crisis Averted! How to Protect Yourself and Your Family from a Financial Crisis

"What is the difference between a taxidermist and a tax collector? The taxidermist takes only your skin."
~ Mark Twain

I'M SURE YOU HAVE heard horror stories of family turmoil and lives ruined due to investment schemes and scams, bankruptcy, outrageous medical bills, identity and property theft, natural disasters, and other unexpected life events. It makes me sick to my stomach to think of some of the possibilities mentioned in this chapter, but unfortunately, as human beings, we have to deal with them. The fact is, whether you are a single person, married, a parent, or you are taking care of other dependents like your aging parents, there are many things you must do to protect yourself and your loved ones in case you find yourself in one of these situations. With proper planning, including allocating some of your income to protect yourself from these situations, you will be much more confident in knowing that no matter what happens, you will be okay. From knowing what key people/experts you should have on your Dream Team, to different types of insurance and things you can do on your own to prevent disasters, let's take a look at how we can protect ourselves and those we love most.

Expecting the Unexpected (Being Prepared When the Unimaginable Happens)

Unexpected life events will always happen, and as much as it sucks to have a wrench thrown into your well-thought-out plans, there are things you can do to alleviate the stress caused by such situations by being as ready as you can be. Or at least be ready for the financial implications of such situations.

To feel comfortable knowing you're ready to handle anything, you need to do these three things:

The Three Ps to Being Ready for the Unexpected

1. Prepare:

The only way to prevent yourself and your family from experiencing financial ruin or crisis due to unforeseen events is to prepare for the worst. The old adage *hope for the best but prepare for the worst* is so fitting here. In no way should the possibility of terrible events run your life and screw up your money mindset. Keeping yourself in the right positive mindset to know that you can get to where you want to be financially, living a life you love, is a big part of all of this. How can you move forward from wherever you are in your financial life now, to be in a better more fulfilling place, if you're worried about what might happen down the road?

More often than not though, people find themselves in

tough situations, and they weren't even aware of the consequences of not being prepared. When determining how to prepare for emergency situations that may unexpectedly come up in your own life, you need to ask yourself, **where do I have risk?**

What personal assets do I need to protect—house, apartment, car, investments, property, your life?

What is my backup plan? Do you have a will, power of attorney, childcare plans, in case of emergency (ICE) contacts?

Do I have the right insurances for myself personally, my business, my home, my health, my children, etc.?

Even now, just briefly thinking about some of these questions at the most basic level, you've probably already started to think of areas in your life where there may be gaps and potential risks to cover. To prevent the effects of these occurrences from putting a major hold on your financial future, it's important to use key people and experts to help you prepare and plan for the worst.

2. Plan:

There are many areas of your life that often require specialized expertise and planning in order to be well prepared for the bumps in the road. To determine what you need to plan for and where you require additional coverage for some of the risks you have identified, it's important to **build your Dream Team.** My Dream Team consists of many experts in different fields including:

- **Financial Advisors**: There are many sources for financial guidance from someone like myself, to the many other online resources mentioned in this book. If you're in the USA and need a financial advisor, look for a fiduciary (see Chapter 7). Choose what best suits your needs.

- **Insurance Brokers**: There are brokers for different types of insurance.

- **Accountants**: Business, personal, or both.

- **Bankers**: I work with people at the bank for banking issues, which are separate from actual financial advisors, registered investment advisors (RIAs), brokers, and fiduciaries.

- **Real Estate Agents**: These experts are a helpful resource when looking at real estate investing options.

- **Mortgage Brokers**: These experts are helpful from a real estate and finances perspective.

- **Lawyers**: Depending on your business and personal situation, a lawyer's expertise is valuable as it relates to your financial plans, and to create your will and powers of attorney over your financial decisions should you fall ill.

It's important to build your dream team on referrals from people you know and trust, and who have used these experts before. Also, be sure to match your needs with those that have the right experience and qualifications. I've almost always received excellent referrals for experts I've needed with the new assets I'm acquiring, or the new risks I'm taking on. Many of these referrals have come from mentors and senior executives I've worked with who have contacts of their own after many years of business and life experience; or they may have friends and relatives who have been through a similar situation in the past. Additionally, a professional already on my dream team may provide a referral.

I've turned to one member of my dream team time and time again for expertise, guidance and advice: my mortgage broker, Pauline Hardy. Pauline is a Senior Mortgage Broker at Invis who was referred to me when I was twenty by my dad whom she's done business with for many years; she provided him stellar mortgage rates for his personal and business needs. Given that I see my father as a highly intelligent and experienced entrepreneur, with lots of knowledge in the field, I trusted his recommendation. Pauline, who I knew was working with many large clients, gladly took me on as a client due to her relationship with my father, his friends, and peers who were also her clients. My enthusiasm didn't hurt, as I was keen to learn about real estate investing, mortgage brokers, and all the ins and outs of buying and selling homes.

As a keen investor herself, we got on like a house on fire (terrible pun for this chapter). Pauline and I would talk on the phone for hours—and I mean hours! She explained everything to me, and truly took the time to make sure I knew what I was getting myself into at such a young age; she helped me find solutions in the very complicated world of mortgages and financing. Through using her as a broker and not going directly to my bank, I was able to secure a fantastic rate on my mortgage—lower than what the bank was offering. The education part of her role is what's so valuable and creates astounding savings. She has helped her clients save and invest tens if not hundreds of thousands of dollars through her ability to change perception on their individual needs and circumstances, such as the pluses and minuses of choosing a variable vs. fixed rate mortgage, refinancing, home equity, and cash for improvements.

Many people are afraid to reach out to brokers because they think it will cost them, that their situation isn't important enough to use a broker, or that it won't be worth their time; in fact, it's quite the opposite. Not only did I receive superior service, education, and savings from using Pauline's services, but I didn't have to pay her a thing since she is paid by the financial institutions and banks that provide the mortgage financing. Pauline even showed up to my housewarming party, gift in hand; she's a true gem! The money she's saved me over the years is incredible, but her genuine keenness to continue her own learning, and help others at the same time, is what really inspired me. Again, the moral of this story is a great referral can go a long way. Pauline and I celebrated our ten-year friendship anniversary this summer, and I hope to have her as a member of my dream team for decades to come.

3. Protect

Cybersecurity

There's plenty you can do all on your own, without expert advice, to protect yourself from an array of potential disasters. A massive issue in today's cyber age is the availability of information online and being susceptible to scams, hacking, and identity theft. Cybersecurity is important because most of our personal information is stored online. Personal and business banking information, credit cards, trusts, lines of credit, mortgages, investments, brokerage accounts, utilities, personal contact information—it's all stored in online accounts. Generations Y and X have mostly gone paperless and do everything online. From our email accounts alone, we've likely sent back and forth enough information to get hacked. But, there's a lot we can do to protect our private and sensitive information.

Protect your passwords and change them often for your online accounts, computers, and phone. Never open emails, click on links, or download attachments if you don't know the sender. Similarly, do not download programs or offers from websites you don't know and trust. I'm probably the furthest thing from a "techie" but I do these things as a basic way to stay protected. There are many free apps like 360 Mobile Security, Avast, SafeTrek, and Prey that help protect your smartphone and tablet devices from viruses and malware, as well as your communications apps, private photos, videos, browser history, tracking, and apps data. These things could all potentially contain your personal information so using such apps and comparable protection services could prevent your information from being hacked and manipulated.

Personal Documents and Irreplaceable Possessions

You should also have a safe and organized way to store all of your important paperwork and irreplaceable possessions. I feel old saying this but everyone has documents and other items that need to be kept safe and secure from fire, flood, and theft. Ever lost your passport or birth certificate? Apartment lease? Car insurance documents? A business agreement or IOU? Vintage jewelry from your grandma? I bet you have! Time to buy a safety box for filing and storage. I bought a SentrySafe filing box from Walmart for $70 about eight years ago when I started accumulating more and more investment paperwork. It helps me stay organized and secure in knowing that my irreplaceable (or costly and painfully replaced) items are as safe as possible from fire, flood, and theft. You should also make copies of these items and store them with a loved one who has a safe place in their home as backup. This isn't high-tech, complicated advice, just simple "adulting" skills!

Ensure You're Insured

I mentioned building your Dream Team and how important these people are to securing your future. Insurance is a huge part of this. Insurance can be a tough subject because there are many different insurance types, plans, premiums, deductibles, etc. Although tackling the subject of insurance is probably my least favorite subject, I do know it's imperative to have some types of insurance incorporated in your financial plan;

I would have been financially destroyed many times without them.

Here is a list of the most important types of insurance to consider:

1. Health
2. Home
3. Renters
4. Car
5. Life
6. Disability
7. Travel

. . . .

Chapter Bonus:

Go to the YFF website to download the **Top 5 Insurances you MUST consider!**

. . . .

Be You and Don't Let Anybody Else Steal "You" Away!

Identity theft is a real thing—super real! I have a friend who actually knows someone with the exact same name, and unfortunately, this other person has terrible credit history. Somehow, over the years, their credit histories got intertwined and the "monkey on her back" has never left. It has taken years for her to straighten out these mistakes with the credit bureaus, stop collection notices and threatening warnings, and restore her credit that shouldn't have been destroyed in the first place. This wasn't a malicious case where the other person was deliberately trying to steal her identity so it's less of a risk, but the damage to her financial independence was the same.

What happens if your credit card numbers or other personal information got into the wrong hands? Always be sure to monitor your credit card statements for charges that aren't familiar; if you have multiple occurrences of different cards or accounts being compromised, you should report it to Equifax, TransUnion, and Experian (USA only) so they are aware that your social insurance/security number and identity may have been stolen and alert you of any suspicious behavior, or potentially freeze your credit. The national credit bureaus also have an option where you can pay a certain amount per month or year to have full access to your credit score and report; this allows you to monitor errors and credit checks in case someone tries to apply for a new card or loan with your information.

Summary

Life's curveballs can be a bitch . . . man do I know it. I can't even count how many sleepless nights I've had over financial, legal, health, and personal safety concerns, thinking the world is crashing down on me and there's no way out. Probably some of the reason why I became so financially aware in my teens and twenties was because I got screwed over many times. From a young age, I've taken a lot of risks, realized big rewards, and also learned many hard lessons (read on in Chapter 10).

Through all the lessons learned and trusted referrals that have come out of the hard times, I've been able to build a Dream Team that provides me with the support, advice, and security I need to comfortably manage my life, investments, and the associated risks. I've also been able to pass along a lot of the skills and knowledge I've gained through these difficult experiences, and the experts who helped me get through them, to my friends, family, and clients. My biggest hope for this chapter and the next is that you will learn from my and others' mistakes, so you can safeguard your own family from the same misfortunes by preparing, planning, and protecting the right way.

My Two Cents:

The Three Ps to Being Ready for the Unexpected:

1. **Prepare: Where's my risk?** (What/who do you need to protect?)

2. **Plan: Build your Dream Team** (Get trusted referrals.)

3. **Protect: What can you do?** (Take action by doing everything you can to protect yourself and your family on your own.)

   - Cybersecurity

   - Personal documents and irreplaceable possessions

   - Ensure you're insured

   - Be you, and don't let anybody else steal "you" away

   - Learn from other people's mistakes

Chapter Bonus:

Go to the YFF website to download the **Top 5 Insurances you MUST consider!**

Chapter 10

Overcoming the Hurdles: Moving Onward and Upward!

"Bills travel through the mail at twice the speed of checks."
~ Steven Wright

LEARNING HOW TO OVERCOME the hurdles on your road to financial independence is key. Every single person on this planet experiences strife, pain, and obstacles to different degrees; in those times you need to remember that **you will get through it** and eventually move onward and upward. As individuals with control over our own money mindsets, bank accounts, and financial decisions, it's up to us, no one else, to make the changes required to live the life we truly want. Sometimes it's tough to see through the shit that falls in your lap and the catastrophes you never saw coming, but there is always an expiration date and a way to move forward. This chapter is most personal to me as I dig deep into some of the issues my good friends and I have dealt with, in the hopes that these lessons will be something you can learn from too.

Developing Your Core Support System

"Life is tough my darling, but so are you."
~ A favorite quote sent to me by three of my core
supporters in a time of need.

A few good friends of mine sent me flowers with the above quote earlier this year. I had just started writing this book when my home was broken into and destroyed—great timing huh? With my home, business, and personal safety at risk, I was in no place to keep writing, be social, or talk to anyone. "Hermit mode" is the term one of these good friends coined, as it's my fallback position when I'm struggling with a business or personal issue I can't get out of my head. The quote resonates so well with me, and many people I'm sure, as it's important to remember during the toughest of times that we all have the choice and ability to be strong-willed individuals. The power in knowing we have the ability to take action and turn things around is what this book is all about.

Roy Aubeelack is one of my closest friends from our London and New York days, and he has supported me through the toughest of personal and business situations. He has overcome his own personal setbacks and difficult family losses at a young age to emerge as a successful investor, intelligent business leader, and most importantly a kind and caring friend. Roy and I have had many discussions about money, investing, wealth, and happiness over the years. Since he became excited about learning the core principles of investing, research, and seeing his money grow through investing in stocks, his personally managed portfolio has returned over 50 percent! Not bad for a guy who has no formal education in finance. He did it and you can too.

I am so blessed to have accumulated a core group of friends like Roy, family members, and mentors over my years in finance thus far that continually inspire me to keep on trekking. They've seen the good, the bad, and the seriously ugly. I mean for real, it's been UGLY at times ... thank goodness these folks helped push me through it.

Having a core support system (outside of your dream team of professionals) to vent to, bounce ideas off of, and provide you with clarity in difficult times is imperative. It's necessary to have professional advice in any given field when it comes to your money, but bouncing ideas off the people who know you best is also important; they might be able to point something out about your personality, risk profile, or lifestyle that you have overlooked while creating your lists of needs and wants and adding them to your Financial Nirvana timeline.

For example, there are many people that tout the need to be entrepreneurial, how fabulous being your own boss is, and that it's the only way to be financially free. This I agree with (for my own specific personality and values), but not everyone is a born entrepreneur and not everyone wants to be. Nor do they have to be! Some people actually enjoy leaving work at 5:00 p.m. and not having to work overtime for no pay on weekends and evenings. The security of working for a well-established company with excellent benefits and a 401(k), or RRSP contribution matching program is often more attractive to many. Having these trusted people in your corner helping you make decisions along the way can make it much less daunting. Your decisions should be based on what works for you.

An exercise to try: Show your lists of needs and wants, and how you've plotted out your Financial Nirvana timeline, to a couple of people in your core group of those you trust and who know you well, and see what they think. You might be missing something so simple you do every day that you hadn't even realized was important to you and your bottom line.

What Doesn't Kill You Makes You Stronger! (Anyone else hearing Kelly Clarkson circa 2011? It's annoying but true.)

When it comes to personal and business experiences I've gone through myself, I am both blessed and cursed in so many ways. It's tough to say whether the terrible things I've been through were truly bad or good. In many ways, I don't think I'd be anywhere near where I am today in terms of perseverance, grit, and knowledge if it weren't for those misfortunes and mistakes. The opportunity to learn from these experiences has paved the way for me to earn more money and make smarter decisions, now and in the future, and has enabled me to share what I have learned with others who are facing similar risks and setbacks.

My first big money lesson was when I was seventeen. I had saved up all year while away at school in Toronto, working three part-time jobs to pay for a portion of my schooling expenses and to save money for a summer car while I was back in Vancouver. I bought the car from a long-time trusted friend who owned a car dealership for $10,000 cash. It was the cutest little blue convertible with a white leather interior; I loved it! The deal was that he agreed to sell the car for me for the same amount at the end of the summer so I would get my money back that I'd saved for school. I'm sure you can guess what happened. I gave him the car back, handed over the keys and he was gone, not to be found until years later. The situation is still unresolved so no happy ending here. Sitting there totally screwed with no money for school, I asked my dad what I should do. In his rational Norwegian style—my dad has always guided me to make clear, educated decisions—he suggested I talk to the bank about getting a low-interest, short-term line of credit; the idea was to get the money I needed to pay for school, while I continued to work my part-time jobs to pay off the line of credit.

The biggest gift my parents have given me was teaching me to be self-sufficient. In this situation, my dad could have bailed me out when times were tough, but instead he showed me how to find a solution. I cried for a while then went straight to the bank and, with my dad as a guarantor, they gave me a $5000 line of credit. Months later, I figured out my "friend" had forged signatures on the sale papers for the car the week after I gave it to him and he had gifted the car to someone else. Unfortunately, the police were of no help and he was nowhere to be found until years later when I ran into him and almost lost it. Lessons learned are priceless!

From this experience I learned:

1) How lines of credit, guarantors/co-signers, and interest on loans work.

2) To never hand over your assets without some form of written agreement.

3) To be wary of people who are all too keen to do you a "favor".

The above is a specific example of someone who intentionally scammed me and was only doing himself a favor, but, sadly, it happens more often than you'd think. This situation deeply affected me mentally and physically, which is almost funny because since then I've been through much worse. Back then, I didn't sleep well for months, and I felt sick to my stomach every day trying to figure out what I was going to do and how someone I trusted and looked up to could hurt me like that and simply walk away. Many of you I'm sure have been through similar experiences of working extremely hard for your money and having it taken away from you unjustly. All the more reason to learn about how to manage your money, prepare for unforeseen events, and be in the right mindset for when shit hits the fan.

Hard lessons from a young age taught me to be wise when it comes to whom I trust with my hard earned cash. Like I said, it didn't end there, far from it; there were many lessons down the road for me: medical bills, health issues, unpaid client invoices in the five-digit range, a major car accident, home floods, personal safety concerns, fraud, and more. As painful as these situations have been to deal with, I always had my core support system steering me ahead.

My dream team of professionals was also pivotal through all of these experiences, as they gave me the education I needed to manage in the moment, and, most importantly, to prevent such occurrences from happening again, potentially at a later stage in life when there's more at risk. My dream team was created through bonding during these hardships, and for that I'm forever grateful. Being on the other side of most of these issues now, I'm constantly running into situations where friends, family, and clients are looking for advice for which I'm more than happy to provide. These things are a part of my history and have made me the person I am today. I'm stronger now than I was before, and I'm all the wiser.

Chapter Bonus:

Go to the YFF website to download your own **Tough Lessons Learned worksheet** where you can analyze your own experiences to bring to light the knowledge and wisdom you gained. Every experience, good or bad, should be a positive learning experience!

From Homeless to $100 Million: If Steve Harvey Can Do It in His Forties, You Can Too!

Did you know that Steve Harvey, the comedic legend and TV powerhouse, was homeless for three years until he got his first major shot at stand-up comedy in his late thirties? I got the chance to meet Steve Harvey earlier this year at a finance and investing conference in Las Vegas, and boy does he have stories. Steve quit his insurance sales job to try to make it as a comedian when he was married with young twins. His comedic ventures didn't take off as fast as he'd hoped, which left him homeless while he tried to make ends meet, sending whatever money he could back home to his family after a falling out with his wife over his risky ventures. For three years, he got by traveling to occasional stand-up gigs in different states, stealing gas for his 1976 Ford Tempo (which he also slept in), and bathing in rest stops and hotel restrooms. He hit his breaking point one day after being stuck in a hotel restroom stall for hours in tears of embarrassment, not wanting to reveal to other patrons the fact that he had been trying to bath himself. Shortly after, Steve got the big shot he'd been waiting for, and the rest is history. Though Steve is a huge success in his own right today, he uses his painful past as motivation to keep moving forward and working both harder and smarter. Steve is a great example of the ability to start over from nothing to chase your dreams at any age. Don't quit now! The best to come might be just around the corner.

A Man I Admire and You Will Too!

A close friend of mine Gabriel Zamora has the most inspiring story of personal and financial triumph of anyone I have yet to meet. Talk about bumps in the road and hurdles;

Gabriel has been through it all and then some. Having never known his father and following his mother's passing from cancer when he was eleven, Gabriel was an orphaned only child living on the streets of Mexico City. While growing up homeless, he met an important young friend, who kindly fed him from his own family's food for many years, who one day told him, "I won't just give you the fish anymore, I want to show you how to fish."

This old saying is one of my own core philosophies on how to teach your children about money and creating wealth. From this lesson, Gabriel began playing a guitar his mother had given him as a final gift the month she passed. He played on public buses for tips in order to support himself. Over a five-year period, he slowly saved enough money for a flight to Vancouver, with $200 left over to get him started in a new life in Canada.

Through his perseverance learning the English language and knocking on doors looking for work, Gabriel found more and more ways to earn money. Being so keen to learn about the film industry, having seen many American films translated to Spanish as a young child, he got his first job in the industry by simply walking onto the set of *The X-Files* in downtown Vancouver one day and asked if he could help. He started that day as a Production Assistant. From there, he gained experience in many other areas of the industry including camera operating, lighting, and he eventually became a producer. He is now a mogul in the Vancouver film and television industry.

Making an income as a producer is just one of his many sources of income, including owning millions of dollars in film equipment assets which he rents out to the industry (following the principle of *investing in assets that work FOR you*). Now forty-three, twenty years after moving to Canada with no family or high school education, Gabriel has a net worth of over $6 million dollars. Gabriel's success story is not only impressive from a financial perspective, but it's extremely moving on a personal level; he has overcome many obstacles when the odds were stacked against him.

A lesson Gabriel hopes everyone will take away from reading his story is that of the compounding effects of achievement. By creating and meeting daily, weekly, six-month, and five-year goals, you're constantly receiving ful-fillment by succeeding, which helps you stay motivated to keep going. Life changes along the way and you will need to adjust your goals, and that's okay. The key is that you keep going. Don't give up! Gabriel sure didn't, and I hope his story will inspire you to keep moving toward your own goals and dreams as well.

Failure Is Part of the Road to Success

The goal of this chapter is for you to reflect upon your own experiences and values to understand common humanity. We all struggle. We all make mistakes. We all feel pain. Shit happens! Beating yourself up and letting the hard times hold you back from the future you deserve is a one-way ticket to misery. A person's true strength is shown in their ability to keep getting back up and moving forward. No matter where you're starting from today, there is a way forward. Only you can change what tomorrow or ten years from now will look like.

Summary

Every time I come across a difficult personal or business situation in my own life, I think of my dear friend Gabriel, and I'm reminded that the path to personal and financial success is a marathon not a sprint. It takes knowledge, action, and, in most cases, exceptional grit and dedication to get there. Learning the language of money and how to attain it is a series of lifelong decisions. Take your first steps now and allow the rest to unfold as you continue to learn and earn more, while saving and spending well. It all starts with you, and believe me it's worth it!

My Two Cents:

- *"Life is tough my darling, but so are you."* When you feel like the odds are stacked and the world is against you remember this. **You are tougher!**

- You need to **develop a core support system** to vent to, bounce ideas off of, and keep you on track during difficult times.

- Learn tough lessons now to reap the rewards later, and don't let fear or past pains hold you back. Hindsight is always 20/20.

- Failure is part of the road to success. Ask any self-made man or woman you admire how smooth their road was and prove me wrong.

Chapter Bonus:

Go to the YFF website to download your own **Tough Lessons Learned worksheet** where you can analyze your own experiences to bring to light the knowledge and wisdom you gained.

Conclusion

*"There is a very easy way to return from a casino with
a small fortune: go there with a large one."*
~ Jack Yelton

IT'S SO IMPORTANT TO remember that we were all
born with the same capacity to learn how to use money as
a tool to be successful in our financial lives. Whether your
parents were rich or poor, educated or uneducated, seasoned
entrepreneurs or worked for minimum wage supporting the
family paycheck to paycheck, we are all born with the ability,
if we choose, to manage our money in a way that works for
each of us. By prioritizing the things we desire most, being in
the right money mindset, and using wise management and
investing strategies, you will get from where you are now to
where you want to be. Start by living within your means. Yes,
there will be some hurdles along the way; but, believe me,
as I sit here watching my dog run around on the beach on a
sunny Wednesday afternoon, free to earn and spend money
as I see fit, the bumps in the road and lessons learned were
worth it.

I've been cashing in on my wise money decisions for many
years now and you can too. When you focus your energy on
spending and saving the money you have now wisely, allowing it to grow exponentially through investing, you have the
ability to meet your future goals while living the good life in

the meantime. Financial wellness is a matter of preservation not deprivation. Spending will always be a series of choices and balances depending on your own true needs and wants, but it doesn't have to feel like you're sacrificing every day to get to some meaningless goal. Get to where you ultimately want to be by implementing the right strategies now.

I hope the ideas and examples in this book have given you hope that you too can reach your own Financial Nirvana. Now that you know what I know, what are you going to do about it? Real results happen through action, and that's why so many people have asked me for help over the years. There's a lot of information here and you may be feeling overwhelmed, but if you don't take action it's useless. Information only becomes knowledge when it's used. When it comes to information that may be foreign to you, like finances, having the information alone isn't enough, otherwise we'd all be billionaires. You need to implement this information which then becomes knowledge. Start by implementing one thing you've learned from this book and celebrate it! It's important to celebrate your wins along the way and congratulate yourself every time you make a positive change in your life that gets you closer to your ultimate goals.

So what's the next step? How are you going to change your financial life and the lives of those you're responsible for? Get going on some of the worksheets and resources I've provided in the **Chapter Bonuses** throughout this book and you will begin to explore your true desires and assess where you are now. Knowing what you're working for is the first step to getting really excited about your future! You can also feel free to reach out to me through **the book's website www. youngfunfree.com**.

I've never been afraid to knock on doors in order to learn more, and that has by far been my biggest asset in becoming financially wise from so young. If you're looking for guidance and support for someone else—whether you're a parent, teacher, or employer—there's a lot you can do to give a leg up to those you care about, to educate and inspire them to make positive changes. I love speaking to young people and professionals about how to get their financial lives in order, as knowing the financial basics now will set you up for the rest of your life. According to PwC in their 2017 employee financial stress survey, *"nearly one-third of all employees report being distracted by personal financial issues while at work, with almost half of that group spending three hours or more each week handling personal finances at work."* If you'd like to try a **Young, Fun & Financially Free workshop** at your organization, please reach out. Whether you're looking to enlighten yourself or someone else, let me know and I'll show you how I can help.

I can't emphasize enough how proud I am of each person reading this book who's looking to actually do something to live a life they value and deserve. Whether you have dreams you never realized were possible, you've been stuck in the doom and gloom of debt for years, are constantly broke, or have an overwhelming fear of all things money related, you're here now, and that's the first step. If you've made it this far I am 100 percent confident you have the grit, intelligence and opportunity to make your ideal life a reality. Think of how much better your life would be if you actually got to live the way you wanted, rather than continuing to fight against whatever it is that's been holding you back!

Or, you might not even know you're stuck yet. If that's the case, please do this exercise to make sure you're on the right path: *envision your life with all the things you need and want now and in the future.* Do you realistically know how you're going to make it all happen? Dollar for dollar? Building a life of value and meaning doesn't happen out of nowhere. You are the only person who can make it happen and, unfortunately, money doesn't grow on trees yet so you're going to have to figure it out one day. The benefits of starting sooner rather than later are endless. Why not now? Start today! I've provided you with plenty of resources to get you started so you're off to the races!

Rolling with the punches is part of life. Let your past mistakes and naivety about money be the driving forces behind achieving your dreams. **The good life is yours for the taking.**

GO GET IT!

References

For a list of further references to statistics and information in this book, please see the *Young, Fun & Financially Free* website at www.youngfunfree.com

Icons in this book were made by Freepik from www.flaticon.com.

About the Author

Leanna founded Black Hawk Financial in 2014 after many years of experience working in diverse niches of the financial services sector worldwide. Her firm consults alongside companies engaged in financial services, alternative investments, media, and technology to create new business and product strategies, marketing initiatives, and to form mutually beneficial joint ventures and alliances. Leanna leverages the breadth of her knowledge and the depth of her networks in the capital markets to deliver high-quality, high-impact solutions to benefit both growing new market segments as well as institutions.

Leanna obtained her financial services regulatory licensing from the FCA UK, graduated with a Bachelors in Business Administration from Ryerson University, and completed capital markets and journalism certificates at Pepperdine University and Harvard. She has achieved this while working and residing in multiple jurisdictions including Canada, the U.S. and Europe. Her entrenched passion for business, travel, acting and modeling has led her to an impressive array of hosting and media accomplishments, seamlessly integrating both her personal and professional interests and strengths.

Leanna is a devoted athlete having been a competitive ski racer, and is a true "give back" enthusiast. She has hosted events and volunteered for multiple organizations including WE, Canadian Breast Cancer Foundation, American Red Cross, SPCA, and The Salvation Army. Leanna is thrilled to be donating 100% of the royalties from "Young, Fun & Financially Free" to the WE movement for the creation of sustainable income opportunities in developing countries.

9 780998 854632